# Classrooms
## Under
### the
# Influence

# Classrooms Under the Influence

## Addicted Families / Addicted Students

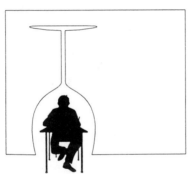

Richard R. Powell
Stanley J. Zehm
Jeffrey A. Kottler

CORWIN PRESS, INC.
A Sage Publications Company
Newbury Park, California

*For information address:*

Corwin Press, Inc.
A Sage Publications Company
2455 Teller Road
Thousand Oaks, California 91320

SAGE Publications Ltd.
6 Bonhill Street
London EC2A 4PU
United Kingdom

SAGE Publications India Pvt. Ltd.
M-32 Market
Greater Kailash I
New Delhi 110 048 India

Printed in the United States of America

**Library of Congress Cataloging-in-Publication Data**

Powell, Richard R., 1951-
    Classrooms under the influence : addicted families, addicted students / Richard R. Powell, Stanley J. Zehm, Jeffrey A. Kottler.
        p.  cm.
    Includes bibliographical references (pp. 148-152).
    ISBN 0-8039-6101-4. — ISBN 0-8039-6102-2 (pbk.)
    1. Students—Substance use. 2. Substance abuse—Psychological aspects. 3. Problem families—Psychological aspects. 4. Compulsive behavior—Social aspects. 5. Problem children—Education.
    I. Zehm, Stanley J.  II. Kottler, Jeffrey A.  III. Title.
    HV5824.Y68P69   1995
    371.7'84—dc20                                              95-23318

This book is printed on acid-free paper.

95  96  97  98  99  10  9  8  7  6  5  4  3  2  1

Corwin Press Production Editor: S. Marlene Head

# Contents

# Preface

Classrooms Under the Influence is a book about addiction, a social phenomenon that influences both social and academic issues in the classroom, is passed on from one generation to the next, and creates challenges for teachers on profoundly personal as well as professional levels. The book is not simply about students who become addicted to chemical substances or alcohol; it is about the complex effects of addiction on the user and the spiraling impact of this addiction on other people in his or her life—family members, friends, and teachers. In every community and in each and every school, there are classrooms under the influence of chemicals, alcohol, extreme lifestyles, and out-of-control behavior of students, parents, stepparents, guardians, siblings, and others within the home. Even when the impact is not directly the result of current addiction, there are enduring effects of past substance abuse by family members.

Even the most dedicated and determined students can be sabotaged by what is going on in their lives. How is a child to do his homework when he lives in fear that his father is about to walk in the door drunk at any moment? How is a child to concentrate in school when her sleep has been disrupted by her parents having another argument about who is most out of control? These children are embarrassed and humiliated, and they choose to remain silent about what goes on in their homes and neighborhoods. And even though what goes on in these environments is not within our jurisdiction or control, our classrooms remain under the influence of these addictions.

We are spectacularly unprepared to deal with these problems. Teachers receive almost no training in understanding the mechanisms and insidious effects of addiction, much less what to do about them. Although we learn quite a lot about how learning takes place and how to function in a classroom as a manager, a motivator, an evaluator, and an imparter of information, we learn very little about how to develop solid relationships with children, how to inspire their trust, and how to recognize their emotional, social, family, and self-esteem problems. We understand very little about what can be done once these difficulties are identified.

How can teachers and schools deal effectively with the addiction phenomenon? How much longer can educators remain in denial of their students' home lives, acting as if the most important thing in the world is what they are doing in class? Perhaps a more pressing and debatable question is, Should schools address the addiction phenomenon in an open manner, especially as it connects to students' parents or other relatives?

Given the prevalence of addiction in our society and its profound influence on classroom teaching, we feel that dealing with problems of addiction openly, honestly, and in a straightforward manner is no longer an option: It is now an educational imperative. We are not implying, however, that teachers should become social workers or counselors in addition to their other overloaded responsibilities. Rather, we are suggesting that by continuing to ignore the impact of addictions in our classrooms, we are making our educational tasks far more difficult. We must address the problems that concern children the most if we are ever to hold their attention to other matters that we consider important. We must educate ourselves about how their lives, and our own lives, are being influenced by substances such as liquids, powders, and pills and by extreme lifestyles such as compulsive exercise or compulsive work, which so distort reality and judgment. Most important of all, we must equip ourselves with the strategies with which we can help to reduce the continued proliferation of addiction in our schools.

**Contents of the Book**

As the title of this book implies, our overall purpose is to pointedly address the issue of addiction, how it affects behavior and dynamics in the classroom, and what teachers can do—both on behalf of children living with addicts and for addicted children. Also included is a discussion of how teachers'proclivities toward addictive behavior may influence their relationships with students and their attitudes toward their work. Building an understanding of how addiction influences classrooms is important for educators everywhere. We have written the book, then, for preservice teachers preparing for the classroom, experienced teachers already in the classroom, other educators such as administrators and counselors, and all other professionals who work with young persons in and around schools.

Building an understanding of addiction involves at least two types of awareness. First, this exploration involves learning how addiction impacts personal lives in profound ways, both in and out of school. This kind of awareness comes through hearing and reading about the lives of persons who live with, or have lived with, addicted persons. We therefore begin the book with our own personal stories of how living with addicted parents influenced our lives at school. These stories demonstrate our personal connection to the subject and provide, we hope, a convincing base for our own expertise as teacher and counselor educators that runs far deeper than intellectual and scholarly inquiry. Each of us has *lived* this book as the survivor of addicted parents.

The second type of awareness is somewhat more familiar (and less threatening). It comes through the intellectual study of the subject—about the prevalence of addiction in our society and about the research that has been conducted on how addiction influences classroom teaching. Beginning in the first chapter, and extending throughout the book, we integrate findings of research reports with actual stories of addiction to develop a compelling case for turning educators' attention to the relationship between addiction and classroom learning.

In the remaining chapters of the book, we follow a template in which we develop a broad and comprehensive overview of the addiction phenomenon as it operates in schools. Chapter 2 provides background information on addiction, addicts, and the sources of addiction (i.e., the substances, chemicals, and lifestyles that provide a basis for addictive behavior). In chapter 3, we describe more specifically how addiction actually affects classroom instruction, not only the behavior of students but also that of teachers.

The addiction phenomenon poses special challenges for all classroom teachers, regardless of their setting, specialty, or grade level. Chapter 4 describes 11 of these challenges that are most commonly at the forefront of our ruminations about our work and also describes our discussions with colleagues about the trials and tribulations of our jobs. In chapter 5, we offer a description of chemically dependent family systems, and we consider how teachers are roped, manipulated, and seduced into the chaotic structures.

Moving into the realm of the practical in chapter 6, we suggest what *not* to do as a classroom teacher with students who are living with addicts and with students who themselves are addicts. Complementing these prohibitions against what teachers do most often that is ineffective, or that even exacerbates problems, chapter 7 discusses the strategies that are considered to be most useful. These represent a state-of-the-art synthesis of what research and practice in teacher, counselor, and therapist education have found to be effective.

Chapter 8 follows with suggestions for making organizational changes to maintain productive and healthy classroom environments in the face of the addiction phenomenon. Specific strategies for identifying and working with children of addicts are provided. Chapter 8 also contains suggestions for developing a classroom plan for assessing, intervening in, and preventing inappropriate behaviors of students who live with addicts. In chapter 9, we close with a return to the beginning, to our own personal stories that precipitated this journey from impairment to high-level functioning—first as students, and then as teachers.

# Acknowledgments

We acknowledge, both regretfully and joyfully, our parents' contributions to our empathy, deep understanding, and experiential knowledge of addiction, which we needed in order to write about this subject with authenticity. They provided us with memories and experiences that are found overtly in the first and last chapters and implicitly throughout the remainder of the book. These experiences, from the worst times of our lives, proved critical as the driving force for our work today.

RICHARD R. POWELL
*Texas Tech University*

STANLEY J. ZEHM
JEFFREY A. KOTTLER
*University of Nevada, Las Vegas*

# About the Authors

**Richard R. Powell** is Assistant Professor of Education in the Department of Curriculum and Instruction at Texas Tech University. He has also taught at the University of Nevada at Las Vegas, Indiana University, and Texas A&M University. Powell has 8 years of teaching experience in middle school and high school settings.

Powell received his Ph.D. in Curriculum Studies from Indiana University, Bloomington. He earned other degrees from West Texas State University, including a B.S. in Biology Education and an M.S. in Biology.

He has been an educational consultant to many government agencies and corporations. He has taught, developed curricular materials, and lectured in the Middle East, Europe, and New Zealand. In addition to his research on teacher development and science education, Powell has coauthored a book with Stanley Zehm on adolescent children of alcoholics. He is currently writing a field-based book for preservice and in-service teachers that will help them develop strategies for teaching in culturally diverse classrooms.

**Stanley J. Zehm** is Professor of Education in the Department of Instructional and Curricular Studies at the University of Nevada, Las Vegas. Prior to his appointment at UNLV, he served as Dean of the Division of Education and Psychology at Heritage College and Professor of Education at Washington State University.

Zehm has 15 years of K-12 experience in public and private schools as an elementary and secondary teacher and school administrator.

Zehm earned his doctoral degree in English Education at Stanford University. He also possesses degrees and specialized training in philosophy, counseling psychology, English, and tests and measurements. He is a licensed counselor and formerly practiced as a licensed marriage, family, and child counselor in California.

He is the author of many articles published in professional journals and recently coauthored a book for middle school teachers and administrators on the identification and treatment of adolescent children of alcoholics. He has also presented workshops to teachers and school administrators on a variety of educational topics and issues in many locations in the United States and Asia. Zehm is coauthor of *Teaching: The Human Dimension*, published by Corwin Press.

**Jeffrey A. Kottler** is Professor of Counseling and Educational Psychology at the University of Nevada, Las Vegas. He has studied at Oakland University, Harvard University, Wayne State University, and the University of Stockholm. He received his Ph.D. from the University of Virginia. He has worked as a counselor and teacher in a variety of settings, including hospitals, mental health centers, preschools, clinics, universities, corporations, and private practice.

Kottler is the author or coauthor of 13 books, including *The Compleat Therapist* (1991), *Compassionate Therapy: Working With Difficult Clients* (1992), and *Teacher as Counselor* (1993, published by Corwin Press).

To our children

# 1

# Lives Outside the Boundary: Stories of Addiction

This book is not only about addiction in the classroom and the effects of self-destructive habitual behavior on children's behavior and attitudes but also about our own experiences. Many of us became teachers not only because we wish to help others but also as a way to help ourselves. If somehow we can draw on what we have learned as the children of addicts, as family members or friends who watched helplessly as those we loved destroyed their lives, or as people who have been addicted ourselves, then the pain seems to have some value.

We will thus be asking you to examine not only the behavior of others, notably children and their parents, but also to explore the origins of your own beliefs, attitudes, and characteristic responses to what happens in your classrooms. Therefore, we can think of no way to approach this subject without encouraging you to explore your own history and experiences with addiction. As you will see, we use this term in the broadest sense of what it means to become overly dependent on a substance (drugs, alcohol, food) or activity (work) in order to function on a daily basis. Our suspicion is that very few of us in this profession, or walking around on this planet, have been able to remain unaffected and unscathed by the effects of addiction, whether directly or indirectly.

Given the parallel focus on the effects of addiction in the classroom, as well as on the ways you personalize this material, we would be somewhat hypocritical if we asked you to do something that we are unwilling to do. This means that because we will be asking you to reflect on your own history and experiences as an addict, as a child of an addict, or as a friend or family member of someone who is or has been out of control, we are sharing the very personal reasons why each one of us ended up collaborating together on a book about addictions in the classroom.

### Richard Powell

I grew up with an alcoholic father and a codependent mother; they were entangled this way as long as I can remember. My father was always the center of attention. When he got drunk, he had our attention in a major way as he tended to become quite violent and physically abusive. This usually resulted in calling my mother ugly names and shoving her into walls.

My mother, my sister, and I lived in constant fear of my father's explosive behavior. We lived his alcoholic life, breathed his drunken breath, and accommodated his stormy and perplexing moods. By the time my mother divorced him, I had spent most of my childhood years under the influence of his addiction. Through all of this, I lived with the constant fear that my father would kill one of us during his rages. Perhaps even more worrisome was the fear that others would learn about our family secret.

All this, of course, cut deeply into my schoolwork. Doing homework was often impossible in the face of Dad's unpredictable drunkenness and fighting between him and mom. I recall very clearly one particular night when I was in the ninth grade. I was trying to do algebra homework when my father came home drunker than usual. I glanced out the window when he arrived, and I could tell he was out of control, stumbling up to the front door. I closed my eyes and stiffened with fear; I knew what was about to happen, like so many nights before.

As he walked in the door, I could hear Mother through the thin walls of our mobile home begin her usual interrogation. With exasperation and despair she asked him, "Where have you been? Who have you been with?" Then their fighting began. I heard him push her against the wall, and she began yelling and crying. She screamed at him to leave and threw his clothes from his closet out the back door.

In my tiny bedroom, I was afraid to move, not wanting to be alive just then; I could feel my heart pounding loudly in my chest. I heard him push Mother against the wall again and again. I finally screamed out loud in my bedroom; nobody heard me. Mom and Dad kept fighting; I ran to the hallway where they were struggling, and I yelled at him to stop, to get out, never to come back. He kept pushing her until she crumbled to the floor, the sound echoing through the paper-thin walls. Finally, he lurched out the door, leaving Mother and me alone in the stillness. She lay on the floor crying; as I stood nearby, my hands were shaking. We said nothing.

The next day, I went to school acting as if nothing had happened the night before, offering no excuse for my unfinished algebra homework. I was scorned by my teacher in front of the class for not doing my assignment, and I was given a zero for my grade. None of my teachers knew what was happening at home; I wanted it that way, and they didn't seem to care.

Although school was hard for me in the face of my home life, I knew I had to finish high school and go to college; it was my only escape, as well as my mother's wish that someday I would achieve something important. I am now living out that dream compulsively, "addicted" to my work, trying to be a family hero, still trying to lift my mother, my sister, and myself above the pain and embarrassment we felt during those many strife-ridden years we lived with one another.

**Stanley Zehm**

On-the-job training was how I gained my first "expertise" with addicted families. As the oldest of four children, it was my regular Saturday evening job to find my inebriated father, bring him home, and sober him up so he could take us to church on Sunday mornings. The successful performance of my task helped us to pretend we were an "all-American family." We pretended so well that not very many people ever discovered our charade. In fact, to this very day, members of my family still maintain our secret. They vehemently deny the extent of my father's problem.

My experience growing up in a toxic family molded my formative years in ways I felt but never understood until years later. I looked forward to going to school each day, especially on Mondays. Now I understand that school provided me with a safe haven I did not have at home. The rules and structure there gave me the boundaries and certainties that I lacked at home. My teachers gave me the adult attention I craved. It did not take me long to learn how to become the subtle, but expert "teacher pleaser." I earned high marks and academic honors, not by pursuing intellectual honesty but by doing everything I could to win teacher approval and attention. I was the teacher's dependable helper. I ran errands, monitored the behavior of classmates, cleaned erasers, collected lunch money, and worked hard at "being perfect."

The pursuit of perfection, begun in my childhood, was a passion of my adolescence as well. I learned how to excel, how to "put my best foot forward." I continued to do well in school, preserving a 4.0 grade point average by avoiding math and the hard sciences. When I entered the Boy Scouts, I was not inspired by the wilderness experiences aimed at male bonding, but by the opportunity to prove myself by winning merit badges and becoming an Eagle Scout. This accomplishment brought me more adult recognition. It helped to hide the pain and embarrassment of our family secret. It also gave me a quasi-military rank that I used to control scouts of lesser status.

Controlling others is critically important to people who grow up in toxic families that are frequently out of control. Very often, it is a form of control that comes in the disguise of messages such as "Let me do that for you," "I only want to help," "Don't worry, I'll take care of you." Armed with such a compelling vocabulary, it is not surprising that I became a teacher. Nor is it surprising that as a teacher I continued the cycle of fostering teacher-pleasing, dependent students. In my classrooms, I unknowingly implemented a culture riddled with floating standards that demanded perfection from a few high achievers and settled for mediocrity from students whom I was caring for instead of teaching.

One day, quite by accident, I was confronted with my family secret. Amid much pain, shame, and sorrow, I began to learn how to end the cycle of addiction that plagues families like mine. I began to rebuild my personal life and acquired a degree of serenity I never dreamed possible. I also began to rebuild my professional life, largely as a result of my willingness to learn from my past in such a way that it stopped polluting the present and future.

## Jeffrey Kottler

I am not an "addict." I have never been addicted to anything except achievement and the compulsive drive to prove I am not as helpless and vulnerable as my mother was. She was an alcoholic.

When I was 13, my mother called me to her bedroom. She had been drinking, which was not unusual for her, but this time her eyes seemed more glazed and her words more slurred than normal. She had probably been taking the pills her doctor had given her.

Even by the standards that I had been used to since my parents divorced, I was completely unprepared for the chilling message my mother solemnly delivered to me. She intended to kill herself that very night. She wanted me to take care of my younger brothers and make everything right after she was gone.

I was in eighth grade, trying to make it through typing class, get my hair to lie straight, and fit into the strange new body and world in which all the rules seemed to change. Yet as important as friends, girls, school, and sports were to me at that time, nothing could come close to my perceived responsibility of keeping my mother alive and my brothers safe.

It was because my mother was an addict that I so strenuously avoided drugs and alcohol when all my peers were smoking dope, dropping acid, and eating magic mushrooms. Control was and is the central theme of my life. Seeing my mother each night, cigarette in one hand, Scotch in another, pillbox open on her lap, and chocolates on the table by the ashtray, forever imprinted in my mind the resolve that I would never become an addict myself. Of course, it took many years for me to put things together enough to figure out why I had been so distracted and lost during most of my adolescence. I barely finished high school, and that only because of the support of a counselor who took pity on me.

There I sat in study hall, when everyone else seemed to have their noses in their books, and I drifted off into my own world. My knee would "accidentally" touch the back of the girl in front of me and I was gone. I would stare out the window as if I was drugged. And in a sense I was, like a crack baby whose bloodstream is poisoned by the indulgences of the mother.

I can now look back over the faces in that study hall, my dear classmates, and realize that in our own ways we were all drugged. We were a classroom under the influence. My best friend was later to die from a drug overdose. My other closest buddy has never come back from an LSD experience; after 25 years he still giggles to himself uncontrollably. So many of us in that room paid scant attention to what teachers were saying. We medicated ourselves for our pain with beer, wine, marijuana, and Quaaludes®. Those few of us who didn't partake were nevertheless casualties from the excesses of our parents who were addicted to their own drugs of choice—Valium®, muscle relaxants, bourbon. It is a wonder that any of us survived.

### An Insider's View of Addiction

Our childhood experiences of living in the households of chronic addicts are, of course, not unique, although as young persons we believed that we were utterly alone in our misery. As we now reflect on our biographies, we are aware of how our home and family cultures of addiction influenced our schoolwork, our relations with peers, and our interactions with teachers. So we, like others who have survived addicted parents or their own addictions, have an insider's view of how classrooms are profoundly influenced by the addiction phenomenon.

It is entirely possible that you may recognize a part of yourself in the pages of this book. If you are one of the fortunate persons who was not bound by the rules and laws of an addictive lifestyle, then this book will help you become increasingly sensitive to what this experience is like for a significant number of your students and peers. And if you are an insider who has felt the impact of addictive patterns, directly or indirectly, you will recognize a part of yourself in the stories that follow.

From our own experiences with addicted parents, as well as the result of years of collective experience in the classroom, we have acquired four levels of sensitivity to this subject.

1. At a personal level, we are intimately familiar with the ways of addiction. We know what children under the influence of an addicted parent feel and do to protect themselves. We understand, more than we would prefer to admit, what it feels like to sit in class, oblivious to what is going on, concerned only with the chaos that awaits us at home.

2. At a theoretical level, we have familiarized ourselves with the research and knowledge base about the addiction phenomenon. We hope to strengthen your awareness and understanding of this subject to the point where you will become more skilled at recognizing the various permutations that indicate when your classrooms are (dys)functioning under the influence of addiction. Such information will be helpful to you, as well, in your attempts to intervene more effectively.

3. As former teachers (Richard and Stan), we know how classrooms are affected by students who are influenced by the addictive lifestyle. As teacher educators and supervisors, we are also aware of how teachers, who are themselves recovering from addictive effects, are functioning less effectively than they could be in

their work with children (Powell, Gabe, & Zehm, 1994; Zehm & Kottler, 1993).

4. As a counselor and counselor educator, I (Jeffrey) have struggled with helping children and their parents work through their problems of addiction, knowing that these are among the most difficult cases for any practitioner to work through successfully (Kottler, 1992). During the past several decades, I have written extensively on personal and professional strategies for intervening more effectively with people who struggle with the effects of dysfunctional families, addictive disorders, and the corresponding assaults on self-esteem (Kottler, 1990, 1991, 1993, 1994; Kottler & Blau, 1989; Kottler & Brown, 1992; Kottler & Kottler, 1993).

Each of these four threads will be interwoven to provide you with a broad perspective on addiction that will equip you with the understanding and skills to respond more effectively to the problems of classrooms under the influence.

## Never Have You Been So Unprepared

With various forms of addiction having reached epidemic proportions in our society, we know that what we experienced in our youth continues to be a significant problem for children everywhere, regardless of race, class, or gender. What is tragic for these young persons, and what prompted the development of this book, is the lack of preparation and education that teachers have in identifying these problems, understanding their effects, and intervening in constructive ways. Moreover, children who live in dysfunctionally addictive environments rarely talk about their home life with anyone, making it even more difficult to provide constructive assistance.

The problem is especially challenging for teachers. Operating as we do in classroom environments where we are responsible for large numbers of students, there is so little time available to monitor the emotional functioning of each child in addition to his or her academic achievement. Some may wonder if this task should even be a part of our jobs. Don't we have enough to do covering the material we are mandated to include in such limited time with such meager resources? Are we not already overwhelmed and overworked with the multitude of peda-gogical, assessment, preparation, and paperwork tasks that we are required to perform? When we are trying to concentrate on planning lessons, presenting units in interesting ways, keeping behavior under control, making reading assignments, and moni-toring progress, how can we function as monitors of emotional stability as well?

Perhaps a more legitimate question would be, How can we not? Of all the roles that teachers serve in a child's life, we take the position that among the most crucial is being a compassion-ate, professional, and sensitive human being who makes the time to check not only on academic performance but also on a child's attitudes, social behavior, and emotional stability.

If just one of our teachers had taken the time to find out why Richard did not complete his assignments, Stan was so obsessed with seeking approval, and Jeffrey was lost in his own fantasy world, our whole lives, most especially our connection to school, might then have changed for the better. In order for this to have happened, however, a teacher would have to have satisfied the following conditions:

1. Made a commitment to invest time and patience to know us, not only as students but as human beings
2. Offered an invitation to us in such a way that it was clear that he or she was accessible and genuinely interested in hearing about our struggles
3. Inspired trust and safety so that we knew that we could talk about our secrets without fear of retribution
4. Demonstrated enough working knowledge of the problems to enable him or her to recognize our behav-ior not as a symptom of laziness or obstructiveness, but of genuine emotional distress that was a side effect of an addictive family environment
5. Acquired skills to reach us in such a way that we would have responded to offers of help

6. Developed the awareness of resources available within the school and community to provide constructive, affordable help to us and our families

7. Shown the willingness to continue an investment of time, energy, and caring in our emotional well-being as well as our mastery of academic tasks

We do not mean to imply that there were no teachers during our whole tenure of studenthood who were caring and interested in helping us; each of us remembers some of these teachers. The problem is that most teachers don't know *how* to help even if they wanted to. How much training have you received in assessing and recognizing addictive and emotional disorders? When a student exhibits atypical behavior or demonstrates evidence of apathy, indifference, obstructiveness, or even excessive approval seeking, how well-equipped are you to figure out what is going on? Even more crucial, how much preparation have you had in what to do about these situations?

## The Pervasive Nature of
## Addictive Effects in the Classroom

One in every four students sitting in your classrooms right now comes from a family in which one or both parents have significant problems controlling their addictions (Tharinger & Koranek, 1988). These students are five times more likely to be victims of sexual or physical abuse (McAndrew, 1985). They have a much higher likelihood of becoming addicts themselves, or of entering into destructive relationships, than do their peers from addiction-free homes (Reynolds, 1987). In addition, children from addicted homes are three to five times more likely to be referred for treatment as learning disabled or behaviorally disordered children (El-Guebaly & Offord, 1977; McAndrew, 1985).

Given that such a high number of students in classrooms today (whether in elementary, middle/junior high, high school, or adult education programs) are struggling under the influence of various intoxicating substances or extreme lifestyles, either their own or their parents', it seems imperative that teachers become more knowledgeable and expert in this area. You have likely had many courses in your subject specialty, in the materials and methods of education as well as the underlying theories of learning, development, and instruction. Some of you have spent years perfecting your teaching style and instructional strategies. But what do you actually know about the mechanisms by which children or their parents become addicted to drugs or alcohol? What do you know about the effects of extreme and compulsive lifestyles of parents (e.g., work, sexual behavior, rage) on your students' well-being? What do you understand about how people under the direct or indirect influence of these addictions are affected in their emotional development, social behavior, and potential for learning? Most important of all, do you know what to do, or not do, when you are confronted with children who are experiencing the negative side effects of addiction?

A child falls asleep repeatedly in your class. Another who has previously been a model student suddenly becomes surly and rebellious. All day long you observe the signs and symptoms of addiction throughout school—students smoking in the bathroom; glassy-eyed zombies shuffling down the halls; neglected, abandoned children whose parents hardly notice the wounds they are inflicting; drug deals being consummated in plain view; overheard conversations of illicit plans for the weekend; beepers going off in your classroom—a sure sign of another drug deal being initiated. You go to the teacher's lounge, and there you see your own peers strung out on their own intoxicants of choice to get through the day—coffee, Cokes®, cigarettes, tranquilizers, chocolate—anything to soothe the stresses and strains of trying to maintain a semblance of order in the face of chaos spiraling out of control.

And there you stand before your students, trying to teach them something about numbers or words or concepts or ideas. You wonder why they don't seem to care. Many are staring out the windows or into the void within them that is filled with pain. It is not so much that they are not interested in learning; it is just that they don't care about what it is that you are teaching them. Talk to them about the transformations going on inside their bodies and lives and you will have their undivided attention. Give them something that works as well as marijuana or beer to soothe their troubled spirits, and you will have them sitting enraptured at your feet. Help them to live with the aftermath of parents who are addicted to vodka, wine, sedatives, or sex, and you will have a most cooperative audience of motivated students.

With addiction prevalent in every corner of our society, there has never been a greater need for you to become aware of the behaviors and heightened emotional intensity of children who are surrounded by lifestyles of addiction. Moreover, with the recognition of the increasing numbers of at-risk students in our schools, more attention is being given to the special needs of students from dysfunctional toxic families (Powell et al., 1994). In addition, children of addiction, whether they are living with parents who are abusing substances or are addicted themselves, are rarely discussed in depth in the at-risk literature (Towers, 1989). They are also underrepresented as a special group to be considered by preservice teachers in teacher education programs and by experienced teachers in in-service seminars and workshops. This is especially disconcerting given the large number of children who carry the addiction lifestyle and culture with them to school classrooms every day.

There are two different ways that children are affected negatively by these experiences. At one level, perhaps a deceptive one for most teachers, they are inclined to become overachievers, not only in school but throughout life (Deutsch, 1982; Towers, 1989). Although this behavior helps some students excel at their schoolwork, those who tend to overachieve often lose their identity in their flurry of nervous energy. This has certainly proven to be the case with the three of us. Our escape from the frustration of our home lives was to excel in the academic world. Although this may certainly be laudable, it has come to us at a dear price. If only a teacher along the way had helped us to understand that there were other things in life more important than achieving As and attaining the elusive goal of perfection. Oh, the things we could have really learned and the fun we could have had, if only we had not been so compulsively driven by fears we didn't know how to effectively deal with. It did not feel like there was a choice in the matter; this drive has become part of our very essence, only now becoming muted by the aging process that, in some ways, can indeed be kind.

Our teachers were most grateful for our compliance. As former classroom teachers, we can think of few things more satisfying than a class of overachieving students, dutifully working on tasks, frowns of concentration etched into their faces. Unfortunately, such behavior, however coveted by teachers, comes with certain side effects for the students. Those who overachieve in school, and who come from an addictive home environment, often report an unusually high degree of feeling inadequate, confused, and angry (Baird, 1991). The overachieving children of addicts often are not sure how to deal with these feelings; they also are not clear about what they have to do with their drive to be perfect. Although overachieving behaviors help these young persons succeed in school, thus masking their feelings of inadequacy, children of addicts are rarely helped to explore their underlying feelings and, consequently, they carry loneliness, anger, and inadequacy into adulthood. They grow up to be adults who may be quite successful, but with certain undesirable attributes that you may recognize in yourself, in our stories, or in the behavior of others.

*Attitudes of perfectionism.* Overachieving individuals often create unrealistic goals, standards for themselves that are impossible to meet. They spend their lives trying to ward off a fear of failure, of not being good enough, of trying to prove to the world that they are really not the frauds that they believe themselves to be (Kottler & Blau, 1989).

*Workaholic lifestyle.* As you are no doubt aware, people can become as addicted to an entrenched pattern of behavior as they can to any chemical substance. A common pattern of behavior often demonstrated by persons growing up in addiction environments is compulsive work habits. Uncontrollable attachment to work has also been linked to high levels of stress and related physical disorders, as well as a propensity toward burnout (Maslach, 1986).

*Need for excessive structure.* One of the characteristics of an addictive home is a notable lack of structure. Such families are characterized as a closed system in which participants conspire together to maintain family secrets (Goldenberg & Goldenberg, 1991). Such environments are typically chaotic, unpredictable, and filled with violence and abuse. In the absence of reliable and consistent structure at home, many children will overcompensate for this loss by overstructuring the ways in which they function on a daily basis.

*Inflexibility in attitudes and actions.* The previously mentioned need for structure also leads to a degree of inflexibility in the way one thinks, feels, and acts. The overachieving adult may find it difficult to deviate from a specific plan or an invariant way of operating. Control becomes a major issue in relationships, often to the detriment of intimacy.

*Lack of perceived freedom and choices.* Implicit in a rigid way of being is a limit placed on what is possible. One teacher described the experience as follows: "I know that I should loosen up a bit. The kids appreciate so much when we deal with something spontaneous, but it just makes me crazy when we fall behind where I think we should be. All the while they are giggling and having fun with some diversion we have gotten off on, I am sitting there thinking to myself how much pressure I feel to catch up. That is the way my whole life feels to me."

*Emphasis on external validation.* There is an overconcern with attaining symbols of achievement—making lots of money, buying nicer cars and houses, winning awards, gaining status. Overachieving adults have lost sight of why they are working so hard to gain accolades or win approval from others. It feels like they are always on probation, always trying to prove their worth to others. Yet what matters most is not what you have accomplished in the past few years but, What have you done lately?

*Risk of physical ailments.* As the past several decades of research studies have indicated, individuals manifesting "Type A," or compulsively overachieving, behavior tend to be more likely to experience strokes, heart attacks, ulcers, and other physical ailments than their counterparts who have a more relaxed, moderated attitude toward life.

*Addiction as self-medication.* It is ironic that in the attempt to prove oneself worthwhile and to escape the legacy of family addiction, the overachiever becomes addicted as well. Racing through life at breakneck speed, such a person may rely on various substances to maintain a productive pace. Coffee, cigarettes, or cola beverages provide boosts of energy at opportune moments. Alcohol, tranquilizers, or sleeping pills are relied on to artificially provide a way to slow down. Illicit drugs such as cocaine, marijuana, and amphetamines are also used by those in high-stress professions in order to function on a daily basis.

We do not wish to disparage the value of achievement. Being and feeling productive is what, in part, gives our life meaning—the belief that we are doing something worthwhile. Rather, we are speaking about what happens when little children are exposed to addictive lifestyles early in life, when the effects of this environment are ignored by educators, and when such children are encouraged to focus on achievement to the exclusion of other aspects of life that are considered necessary for a healthy lifestyle.

### The Other Side of the Coin

The second way in which children from addictive environments may adapt is by developing an underachieving style. This is especially the case when those who are unable to compensate for low self-esteem and poor self-images withdraw from classroom activities and don't work up to their potential. Underachievers might not always carry their quiet, withdrawn, aloof behavior into adulthood, but while they are in school this behavior ultimately keeps them marginalized; that is, on the periphery of academic and social life at school.

Underachieving students do get through school, but their preference is to be seen and not heard; in fact, some of these persons prefer not even to be seen. For example, whereas Richard and Stan adapted to their emotional traumas by overcompensating to prove their value to themselves and others, Jeffrey became a stellar underachiever: "I was teased constantly by my friends and family that I would not graduate high school, much less ever get into college. I was always a mediocre student, a level of performance consistent with my view of myself—an ordinary, inadequate, talentless young man who was heading nowhere. My teachers did not notice me; I was invisible."

Underachievers exhibit characteristics that you will most likely recognize all too well, if not in people you are close to, then in many of the students you see every day.

*Lack of personal initiative.* Whereas overachievers set unrealistic goals for themselves, underachievers rarely set personal goals at all. Rather than become a hero by accomplishing multitudes of superhuman goals, underachievers would rather not accomplish anything that might put them in a position of visibility. Setting and achieving even small goals would give underachieving students more attention than they want.

*Tendency to withdraw.* To maintain feelings of loneliness and inadequacy, underachievers withdraw from most social situations. They are often viewed as being shy, quiet, and afraid. Whereas overachieving individuals tend to adopt workaholic lifestyles, underachievers who withdraw seek less visible lifestyles among peers at school and in social settings outside school.

*Apparent lack of structure.* Underachievers often need structure and clear guidance to accomplish even the smallest tasks. Yet they tend to shy away from both structure and guidance. Although these persons are often very capable of creating their own structure, their lack of personal initiative, combined with being withdrawn, provides them with no real need for structure. This lack of structure places underachieving students outside normal classroom activities where they feel safe and not threatened.

*Excessive compliance.* Whereas overachievers are highly inflexible in thought and action, underachievers tend to be completely flexible, displaying what we interpret as excessive compliance with authority. This compliance, however, results from a lack of personal initiative and unclear personal goals, and it is grounded in feelings of fear and inadequacy. For underachievers, being overly flexible and compliant should not be viewed as a positive attribute, but rather as a way to accommodate inappropriate feelings learned at home.

*Avoiding responsible choices.* Underachievers and overachievers are similar in their tendency to avoid responsible choices. Overachievers avoid choosing between options because of their self-imposed rigid structure. On the other hand, underachievers avoid choosing between options as a function of their self-imposed lack of structure. Not making choices is one way for these persons to protect their preferred place on the outside of social events and classroom activities rather than the inside.

*Avoiding validation.* Overachievers rely on symbols of achievement for personal validation. Underachievers may actually avoid these symbols. Finishing class assignments on time, getting good grades, and participating in many school activities are all ways to validate the self in the school culture. Feeling inadequate and rejected at home, underachievers avoid the very symbols that define success at school and that provide sources of acceptance and validation of their adequacy.

## Our Stories Revisited

We began this chapter with a brief description of our lives in homes that were ruled by parents who were addicts. Apropos of our discussion about overachieving and underachieving students, two of us (Richard Powell and Jeffrey Kottler) were very clearly in the latter group during our precollege years. Trying to survive at home, we had little time or energy remaining to focus our attention on schoolwork. Richard, for example, was placed in a low academic track in junior high school and ultimately graduated in the lower one third of his high school class. Not until his first year of college did he begin to exemplify the characteristics of an overachiever both in and out of school. He became compulsive about making perfect scores, worked constantly to attain success, and sought validation in excellent college work.

A similar scenario unfolded for Jeffrey as well. It was not until his second year of college that he began to blossom. One teacher in particular noticed something in Jeffrey that was worth nurturing. Jeffrey recalls, "Once the teacher began to believe in me, I started believing in myself as well as pleasing others in positions of authority." The balance of Jeffrey's adult life has been spent doing just that—striving for higher levels of achievement and validation in order to prove his essential value as a human being.

Stan, on the other hand, has almost always demonstrated characteristics of an overachiever. He learned quite early in life what it took Richard and Jeffrey longer to realize: As long as we please our teachers and keep them happy, we don't have to undertake the more difficult task of finding our own way in life.

### Summary

This book is about students in your classroom who are growing up in a family with an addict—often a parent, a guardian, or a sibling. The book is also about children who have accommodated to their personal worlds by becoming addicts themselves. In some ways, this book is a symbol for what a portion of our society has become: adults and children who are out of control, who seek to anesthetize themselves from the pain and uncertainties of daily life, who prefer to hide rather than face their struggles directly.

Children living with addicts are driven by uncertain feelings and emotions that are manifested in socially and academically self-defeating behaviors. Whether you now live with an addict or have lived with one in the past, the addiction phenomenon touches your life socially and economically. In your professional life as a teacher, addiction influences the interactions you have with many of your students, the environment of your classroom, the level of your instructional effectiveness, and the social dynamics among your students. As our own biographies suggest, and as the lives of millions of other persons reveal, no classroom, no teacher, no student, either directly or indirectly, is ever entirely free from the influence of addiction.

# 2

## Shields and Bucklers: What Teachers Should Know About Addiction

Addictions come in a variety of forms, including liquids (alcohol), substances (drugs), behaviors (gambling, overeating), and other self-destructive activities. In all their various manifestations, addictions are characterized by a number of features: (a) a repetitive pattern that increases in frequency; (b) a lack of personal control over the activity; (c) negative side effects that impair functioning; (d) combined biological, psychological, sociological, and behavioral components; and (e) a tendency to reinstate the behavior after temporary abstinence (Donovan, 1988). In simple terms, addicts are persons who are unable to stay away from their self-abusive patterns and habits, regardless of the consequences.

### What You Already Know

Most of us already know quite a bit about addictive processes, and much of this knowledge comes from personal experience. We have all experienced, at one time or another, the compulsion or intense craving to engage in some activity that we know is not particularly good for us. In spite of promises that we have made to ourselves, or the best of intentions, we ignore our good sense and indulge ourselves anyway, often without conscious thought. This phenomenon is easily evident in the ways that people drink coffee, smoke cigarettes, or engage in other socially acceptable addictions.

The issue is not, therefore, whether we are addicted to something, be it compulsive exercising, Coca-Cola®, frozen yogurt, or serial sexual relationships, but the extent to which this behavior is self-defeating. For example, the person who absolutely must have a beer, a glass of wine, or a cocktail before dinner every night, or who simply cannot go to bed at night before indulging in a nightcap, is clearly an addict in the sense that choice has been abandoned in favor of regimented obsessive habits. The critical question, however, is, What effect does this addictive behavior have on this person's healthy functioning? Surely it is no big deal to have a glass of wine each evening; there is even evidence that it may actually prevent certain health problems such as heart disease and strokes. What, then, of two glasses, or three, or seven? At what point do we draw the line? The simple answer is when this behavior not only ceases being a choice under your control but there are observable side effects that impair your ability to function. If, for example, you develop a craving for that glass of wine and you cannot relax or sleep without it, then there is an addictive problem.

Addiction is hardly a dichotomous, all-or-nothing condition, which a person either has or does not have. Rather, addictive behavior falls along a continuum resembling a model suggested by Lewis, Dana, and Blevins (1994), where on one end there is complete abstinence, and on the other end is dependence on the substance or activity to the point where health is threatened. In the middle areas would fall moderate use that is not problematic and heavy use that creates serious problems but is less than a full-fledged addiction.

At each point along this continuum, an assessment needs to be made to determine the extent to which the potentially addictive behavior is disruptive and problematic. Obviously, self-report by the user alone is hardly sufficient because the user's behavior may be more a problem for family members or co-workers than it is for him or her. Most assessments on the extent of addiction are therefore typically made through consensus by the identified addict, family members, and the professional involved in the treatment.

As we warned you, much of this you already know. It makes sense that addiction is not a single category. It also seems apparent that the addict's own opinion of the situation may be somewhat different from others who must live or work with him or her.

Your personal experiences with addiction go far beyond your own domain, for it is likely that you have known people (or know them now) who struggle with addictions with more dramatic proportions than those we have mentioned thus far. Almost every one of us has encountered close friends or family members, colleagues or acquaintances, whose lives have been destroyed by their addictions to drugs, alcohol, gambling, promiscuity, or overeating. We have witnessed marriages ending and families falling apart. We have watched people we love spin completely out of control, apparently powerless to take charge of their lives. We have experienced, firsthand, the incredible feelings of frustration and helplessness in trying to reach out to these people. We have listened to their promises and heard their pleas for just one more chance. We have stood by, aghast at the level of depravity to which they have slipped. We have shaken our heads in utter disgust at how low some people can go in the pursuit of their addictions.

You are also well aware of the costs of addiction. You know that it causes harm in innumerable ways, that it is destructive to families, and that it costs society unimaginable sums of money. With respect to alcohol abuse in the United States alone, it has been estimated that the fiscal damage runs into the hundreds of billions of dollars. Furthermore, alcohol is a factor in half of all accidental, homicidal, and suicidal deaths (Wodarski, 1990). You have read about the costs to industry and the health care system of trying to minimize the deleterious effects of addiction—the resulting health problems, the absenteeism from work, the industrial accidents, the lying and deceit that often accompany the continued abuse.

The purpose of this chapter is to build on what you already know, to supplement your knowledge in such a way that you can recognize more easily which of your students is headed for trouble. By deepening your awareness of addiction, you will also become better prepared to deal with related issues that arise in your classroom.

## Addiction as a Family Process

Persons who are unable to make rational decisions about using substances (e.g., drugs and alcohol) or about participating in compulsive behaviors (e.g., gambling, eating, sex) have become addicted psychologically and/or physiologically. When these persons live with others at home, the irrationality of the addiction becomes part of the thinking of all family members. That is, the addiction, as a psychological or physiological phenomenon, becomes a family process. And whether they want to or not, family members are involved in perpetuating the disease, especially when the addiction has been ongoing for many years.

The term *enabler* is commonly used to describe persons who either explicitly or implicitly help someone to maintain an addictive lifestyle. For example, a man complains incessantly that he no longer finds his wife attractive because she overeats. Yet every time she tries to go on a diet, he unconsciously sabotages her efforts by stocking the shelves with exactly the same foods that are her greatest temptation.

Another common scenario involves a young girl who has become a daily user of marijuana. Although her parents express their concern over her increased lethargy, indifference, and mood swings, they continue to supply the opportunity (leaving her alone for long periods) and the resources (leaving money lying around) for her to easily continue her destructive behavior.

When addiction is treated as a family process, rather than simply the problem of an individual, the identified patient may be the symptom of underlying dysfunctional patterns. It is for this reason that the standard operating procedure for a therapist working with an addicted child (or one with any emotional problem) is to first ask to meet with the parents in order get some background information. Often it is unnecessary to even see the child because the actual problems may reside more legitimately in the relationship between the parents.

Not only is the addict's behavior driven by problems that occur within the family system, but conversely, this person also attempts to control and manipulate the behavior of others. In fact, addicts are usually quite cunning in their ability to train others to enable their continued addictive behavior. For instance, a mother tells her child that she does not really have a drinking problem; she just likes a few glasses of wine every day to help her relax: "Would you mind, honey, telling your father you'd like to go out for dessert? While you're out, maybe you could ask him real nice to bring me back a bottle of that Chablis I like so much. That's a darling! Come here and give your mother a hug!"

In order for almost any addict to continue with behavior that is disruptive to the lives of so many others, a conspiracy of cooperation among family members, friends, and even personnel in the school is required. The disruptive behavior is ignored, inadvertently reinforced, or encouraged by others who enjoy the benefits of having a scapegoat. As one ex-addict explains, "Yeah, sure, they [my family] complained about me all the time but they sure made it easy for me. My younger sister had a field day As long as I got my parents' attention then she could get away with murder. That's why she used to cover for me. Even my parents were such hypocrites. All the time they told me that coke [cocaine] was so bad for me, they were doing their own stuff. My dad likes his brandy. Mom has been taking Xanex® or some tranquilizer ever since I can remember. And where the hell did they think I got the money to buy the drugs?

"Once I got clean it became apparent how much they needed me to be their problem. I was their distraction. After I got my act together, then they got a divorce. All those years, I think I was the only thing keeping them together."

In a discussion of children of addicts, Towers (1989) mentioned several rules that sustain an addictive family environment, at least with respect to alcohol abuse. We have adapted these rules to fit addiction in general. Each of them illuminates how addictive behavior is maintained through the active participation of all family members.

*The addiction is the central feature of the family's life.* Anyone who has lived with an addicted person can tell you how involved all family members ultimately become in the dysfunctional behavior. No one at home is free from the controlling and/or demanding behaviors of the addict. If, for example, a mother is drunk and violent again, then children at home are afraid, angry, and anxious. When she passes out, the children then feel abandoned and rejected.

*Someone or something else caused the addict's dependency; the addict is not responsible.* Addicted persons deny they have a problem; when that does not work, they refuse to accept responsibility for what is going on. It is always someone else's fault or the result of forces that are beyond their control. In one book about the tendency of such individuals to engage in blaming versus changing, the following excuses are often offered (Kottler, 1994):

- I didn't do it.
- I wasn't even there.
- I couldn't help it.
- I didn't mean it.
- She asked for it.
- I was just kidding.
- It wasn't me, it was the . . .
- It wasn't a big deal.
- I had no choice.
- It runs in my family.
- Nobody told me.
- I didn't know the rules. (pp. 84-85)

In each case, the person seeks an excuse that will absolve him or her of responsibility. Such excuses include having too much stress at work, an important business arrangement that fell through, or a relationship with another person that caused tension again. Addicted parents are also quick to find fault with their children, yelling at them inappropriately for small problems, which provides them with an excuse for turning to their addiction. In these instances, children feel guilty for appearing to be the source of the parent's drinking.

*The status quo of the home environment must be maintained at any cost.* Addicts strive to control everyone at home, thus maintaining a closed environment. This is particularly problematic for young adolescents, who need to develop personal autonomy and a sense of self but who also need a degree of structure and limit setting.

Addicted parents don't allow this natural development to occur for their children. Adolescent children of addicts aren't allowed much personal freedom at home; they must yield to the needs and demands of the irrational parent. This eventually may cause adolescents to develop an inappropriate dependency on their parents; they are often unable to free themselves of this learned dependency later in life when they try to establish a meaningful, wholesome relationship with another person.

*Everyone at home is an enabler for the addict.* In unique and distinctive ways, every family member inadvertently helps the addict keep the addiction alive. These enabling roles learned at home stay with family members when they go outside the home. This is especially true for children and adolescents, who take these behaviors to the classroom with them, recruiting their peers and even their teacher as coconspirators (see Deutsch, 1982; Powell et al., 1994).

*No one may discuss what's really going on with the addiction, either inside or outside the home.* Denial is a salient feature of addicts and their families. Family secrets are pervasive in an addicted home. Members attempt to disguise or hide the deviant behavior; they don't want others to know there is a problem, and family members will often pretend to one another that everything is just fine. Nobody mentions to Dad that they heard him stumble in drunk the night before. Nobody mentions they saw Mom passed out on the bed. Moreover, the embarrassment and shame many young persons feel about their addicted parents also keeps them in denial of the problem.

*No one can say what they are really feeling.* Expressing feelings, saying that "I'm angry about your drinking" or "I'm afraid when you pass out," is against the rules of the addict. Indeed, expressing these feelings would be crossing the boundary of denial and altering the status quo at home. Children of addicts learn to keep their feelings to themselves. That these persons have difficulty with intimacy later in life and are unable to deal with emotionally charged situations effectively or appropriately is not surprising.

To replace these rules of the addict with more appropriate patterns of interacting with family members requires far more than that the addict give up booze or go to Sex Addicts Anonymous meetings. By the time the addiction has matured, family members have learned to suppress emotion, hide anger, live in denial, and jump at the whims of the addicted family member. All these interactive patterns must be changed over time. And because old habits have a propensity for stability, much effort must be made by all family members to overcome inappropriate codependent habits.

## Why Students Use and Abuse Substances

Probably the single dumbest question a teacher or parent has ever asked a child is, "Why do you use drugs?" The answer is as predictable as it is accurate: "Because it feels good!" And this child is absolutely correct: Nothing works better than alcohol or drugs to give a person instant relief, immediate escape from one's problems, and an unparalleled feeling of well-being. Just take a pill, drink a few beers, smoke some pot, and—voilà!—the world looks a heck of a lot better. You see, the problem is not so much the drug experience itself, which is most pleasant, but the side effects that come afterward.

If we took a poll of the readers of this book, we're sure that the majority of you would have tried or experimented with illicit drugs at least once or twice in your lives, and almost everyone has used legally prescribed drugs, alcohol, coffee, or tobacco products. In his study of mind-altering experiences across cultures, Weil (1972) observed that there is no culture ever discovered on this planet that has not had institutionalized drug use (except the Eskimos because it is too cold in their territory to grow anything). That makes most of you users of substances. The question that surfaces from this, then, is, For what reasons did you use (or abuse) illicit substances in your youthful school days? Were you a habitual user of licit substances? We're confident in predicting that the answers you give to these questions will be similar to answers young people give today for using both licit and illicit substances.

In the summary below, adapted from material developed by Kottler and Brown (1992, p. 251), we present many of the reasons why children both use and abuse drugs:

| Why Children Use Drugs | Why Children Abuse Drugs |
| --- | --- |
| Euphoria | Biochemical predisposition |
| Boredom | Physical addiction |
| Rebellion | Habituation |
| Curiosity | Addictive personality |
| Pain suppressant | Social reinforcement |
| Peer pressure | Impulsivity |
| Social lubricant | Poor self-esteem |
| Enhancement of reality | Escape from reality |

It is evident from this summary of factors that the distinction between use and abuse is often mediated by personality, biological, familial, and environmental characteristics within each individual. Two children may start out snorting a line of cocaine out of initial curiosity. One shrugs to him- or herself, indifferent to the experience, wondering what the big deal is other than a runny nose and sense of numbness. The other soars immediately into the ozone. Their initial expectations, family history, and certainly their biological constitutions all play a part in determining for each individual a unique set of reasons why substance use or abuse continues.

### Reasons for Widespread Use

*Licit drug culture.* Young persons have reasons, other than because it feels good, for using and abusing substances. Before talking about the specific reasons young persons give for using substances, we need to emphasize that one overarching reason for widespread use of substances is that all corners of our society are permeated by a pervasive and ever-present drug culture. As Kottler and Brown (1992) noted, the United States is a culture centered on drug use. From coffee, tea, and sugared drinks to over-the-counter sales of licit drugs, we spend billions of dollars annually on substances for stimulation, medication, and relaxation. As a society, we use drugs to start our bodies up in the morning, ease the afternoon headache, and escape from the day's stress in the evening. Few of us are free from the stronghold that chemical substances have on our lives.

*Mass media.* The susceptibility of young persons today to using mood-altering substances, most especially alcohol, is made more likely by the influence of mass media and advertising. Advertisements for alcoholic beverages (e.g., beer, wine coolers) are found everywhere. You only have to glance around when you drive home from work to see these seductive messages on billboards, turn on the radio to hear them, and watch a few minutes of television to see more of them. These advertisements, which suggest that drinking alcoholic beverages is socially and culturally acceptable, masquerade beer as a soft drink and depict drinking as the way to fit in with the incrowd. By the time children grow into adolescence, they have seen thousands of beer commercials, especially if they watch sports on television.

The cumulative message from all this is that it is OK to drink alcoholic beverages and that you will have lots of fun doing it. What the advertising fails to reveal, however, are the hundreds of thousands of deaths related to alcohol each year, the stunted emotional development that occurs in young persons who frequently use it, and the potential it holds for abusive patterns of consumption.

## Reasons for Use and Abuse

The effect of mass media on the images that young persons have about themselves as drinkers and the fact that North

American society is permeated by a licit drug culture are two factors that influence the widespread use of drugs and alcohol by both adults and children. These factors also provide a sociological and psychological foundation for the reasons young people give for using drugs. Using recent reports on substance use by children and adolescents (e.g., Johnston & O'Malley, 1986; Novacek, Raskin, & Hogan, 1991; Walter, Vaughan, & Cohall, 1991), we have compiled a list of the common reasons young people use substances.

*Belonging.* One of the most common reasons students give for using substances is to belong to a peer group and to have a good time with friends (Johnston & O'Malley, 1986). This is particularly true for middle school students who, as early adolescents, have a strong need to be accepted socially and to belong to peer groups (Novacek et al., 1991). Middle school and high school students are equally susceptible to substance use and abuse, but middle school students are particularly vulnerable given their emerging need for social engagement and belongingness. What is important to note is that mass advertising campaigns, especially for beer, depict young adults associating with peer groups.

*Experimentation.* Many students try licit and illicit substances, including beer and other alcoholic beverages, just to see what they are like. They often wonder, What is the big deal anyway? Why do adults invest so much time and energy trying to convince us to stay away from this stuff? There is a lure to discover the forbidden.

Students who experiment, however, do not always become abusers of drugs. In fact, many of you reading this book experimented only once or twice with an illicit substance and yet did not become a heavy user or an addict. Experimentation is, nonetheless, the first step to altering moods, escaping the immediate reality, and discovering the heightened emotionality of substance use.

*Coping with problems and troubles.* If some of your students are growing up in dysfunctional families, then they are more likely to use and abuse substances than students who are not exposed to this toxic environment or to develop extreme lifestyles in adulthood such as workaholism (e.g., Deutsch, 1982; Hernandez, 1992; McKay, Murphy, McGuire, Rivinus, & Maisto, 1992; Priest, 1985; Sanders, 1989; Walter et al., 1991). Faraco-Hadlock (1990) noted that dysfunctional families actually push children toward addiction and codependence. Persons living in dysfunctional family home environments complain more often of emotional pain, anxiety, anger, and fear. Heavy users cite these very reasons for using with greater frequency than other students (Johnston & O'Malley, 1986).

*Emerging adulthood.* We have already pointed out how alcohol is portrayed as an acceptable part of our society. It is part of religious ceremonies in some churches. It is often found at festive occasions such as weddings and graduation parties. Alcohol, in the form of toasts, is also used to commemorate special events, such as dinners and award ceremonies.

As your students grow up, they watch adults in all these situations use, and in some instances abuse, drugs and alcohol. This suggests to young persons that they can use substances openly in their lives. In fact, one of the time-honored celebrations for some young adults on their 18th or 21st birthday is go out with friends and legally get "smashed." Students, then, grow up with, and are surrounded by, substance use and abuse by their adult role models. These same youngsters, by living in substance-using home environments, are habituated to life patterns of use before they are able to make informed decisions about drinking and before they go out to live on their own.

*Genetic and environmental predispositions.* A few studies suggest that some students, especially those whose parents have become addicted to alcohol or illegal drugs, are genetically predisposed to becoming addicts (Faraco-Hadlock, 1990). Although it is difficult to resolve the old debate about whether environment or heredity plays a bigger role in developing addictions, there is no doubt that both elements play a role.

When children are genetically and/or environmentally predisposed to addiction to a substance, they begin drinking rather innocently, perhaps to experiment with friends or to be accepted by a peer group. Soon, however, they no longer drink because they want to; they drink because they have to.

*Other reasons for use and abuse.* We have briefly described five key reasons why students in your classes use and abuse substances. These reasons are based on sociological, familial, and developmental considerations. There are also many other reasons that have been reported—as an anecdote for boredom, as a method of relaxation and stress reduction, as a means for dealing with negative emotions, as a temporary boost to self-esteem and confidence, and even, most of all, because it feels good. It is because there are so many "hooks" that attract and maintain addictive behavior that your task of helping these children is made so much more difficult.

## The Stages of Addiction

Not every one of your students who experiments with alcohol or illicit drugs becomes addicted. Indeed, by the time your students finish high school, a very high percentage of them will have tried alcohol, and a moderately high number will have used marijuana several times (Johnston & O'Malley, 1986). How, then, does a student become addicted to substances? What are the stages of addiction that students experience? How can you, as a teacher, recognize students who are becoming addicted?

Gabe (1989) described four phases of substance addiction, each of which progressively follows the previous one. These include the following stages: (a) experimental use, (b) social use, (c) abuse, and (d) chemical dependency.

### Phase 1: Experimental Use

A very high percentage of students experiment with various licit and illicit substances before they graduate from high school. Starting at an early age, most of your students will experiment with alcohol and marijuana before they reach the

10th grade, and some will try cocaine, LSD, speed, and PCP before they graduate from high school.

In this experimental stage, students use alcohol and drugs only occasionally, possibly at a party with friends or just out of curiosity. This kind of use usually does not impair academic performance at school, and students who only experiment do not use drugs at school or at home. In fact, parents and teachers probably will never know about this exploratory behavior.

Experimental use is most often linked to students' needs to fit into a peer group, to be accepted by friends, or to have a good time with friends. That is why experimental use occurs with friends and not while alone. However, experimental users learn that they can alter their moods with drugs, and the payoff for students who have ongoing tension and anxiety is great. Once a substance has been tried and curiosity has been satisfied, some students choose not to continue using or to try again. For others, however, the need to be part of a peer group or the lure of escape from anxiety and tension is an invitation to return to the euphoria and momentary bliss brought on by using the substance.

### Phase 2: Social Use

The second phase described by Gabe (1989) is called social use and refers to the behavior that may take place at parties and other social gatherings. Students begin looking forward to socially using drugs and alcohol to alter moods and to have a good time with friends. It is at this point that substance use begins to be a regular part of a student's life.

Children who have learned that substances can temporarily increase their self-esteem or eliminate anxiety begin planning to indulge during specific weekend situations with friends. Some young persons begin buying substances to save for the next planned event where use will occur. Social use gives students firsthand experience with tolerance when they consume too much alcohol and become ill.

During this stage, you may begin to notice the first signs of impairment, at least with respect to attitudes toward school. Homework and test performance may decline. Students who previously have been cooperative may begin to display discipline problems, withdrawal, or tardiness.

At home, social users begin lying to parents about their use. They hide drugs at home and get into their parents' liquor cabinets. As the need increases to keep their social use a secret, such young people begin withdrawing from family members and family events to be with their friends who also use.

### Phase 3: Abuse

If social use continues for prolonged periods, your students will become psychologically dependent, a state in which the behavior has become habitual. Their school grades drop off considerably, and their peer group often changes to one that involves a drug-using subculture.

During the abusive stage, students increase both the frequency and the amount of use. They use "harder" drugs and drink stronger alcoholic beverages. They become increasingly preoccupied with their drug of choice and begin using substances at unpredictable times, often when they are alone.

Grades show a significant drop because the student is under the influence at school. Short-term memory is impaired, and lack of motivation to learn causes discipline problems. Attention span is reduced, and participation in class activities becomes limited. Abusing students drop out of extracurricular activities. These students exhibit increased behavior problems, including fighting, obscene language, defiance, and negative attitudes toward school (and teachers). Mood swings are more prevalent, and the effect of the substance abuse causes depression in these students.

Abusing students isolate themselves more from family members, and they are no longer fearful of coming home under the influence. They begin stealing money from family members and take liquor from home. Parents become disconnected from their abusing child; they don't know their child's friends anymore, and parents are kept at a distance.

### Phase 4: Chemical Dependency

The final phase is characterized by a chemical dependency, or actual physiological addiction, complete with withdrawal symptoms if the person attempts to stop. This makes the likelihood of ceasing the behavior much less possible and presents a much more difficult treatment challenge.

Students who are chemically dependent spend much of their time alone using their drug of choice (or what they can afford or is available). Drugs or alcohol no longer serve a social function but have become central to daily life. These students are frequently absent from school, and some drop out of school altogether. Others are pushed out of school because of their involvement with classroom disruptions and/or ongoing absenteeism. When your chemically dependent students do attend class, they are probably under the influence.

Trouble at home is also expected when adolescents abuse substances. The abuse becomes a family disease, and all members of the family become involved either directly or indirectly with the abuse. The abusing adolescent tends to hang around only with peers who are also heavy users and who have a mistrust of others. Social experiences become exclusively drug related. Emotional development is severely retarded. Some abusers think they are going crazy and may attempt suicide. Severe mood swings and depression occur.

When students reach the abuse stage, they have become turned off to school, their families, and normal adolescent activities. Their peer group has become highly selected and private. Abusers distrust adults and are protective of their addictive habit.

## Types of Frequently Used Substances

The critical age span in which students are most likely to begin experimenting with drugs is between 13 and 16 (Segal, 1991). Indeed, it is almost a rite of puberty to begin this exploration. Experimental or habitual use may begin in the middle school years, but the percentage of students using substances such as alcohol and marijuana on a weekly basis increases significantly from middle school to high school. In one study that took place in a rural school district, Novacek et al. (1991) found that 5% of middle school students used alcohol weekly, whereas that percentage jumped to 19% in high school. In urban schools, those figures are considerably higher.

Although a high percentage of young people abuse alcohol and marijuana, there are quite a number of other substances on the scene as well. We briefly describe the most prevalent drugs so that you may familiarize yourself with signs and symptoms to look for in the behavior of your students, as well as the jargon that is part of this culture.

## Alcohol

America's love affair with alcohol is ever present; from 1976 to 1984, alcoholic beverages were tried at least once by over 90% of the student population. Even more alarming, a full three quarters of the children who drink alcohol do so in order to have a good time with their friends (Johnston & O'Malley, 1986).

Although alcohol may be one of the most common substances used in our culture, it is also among the most dangerous in terms of addictive effects. Like other central nervous system depressants, an overdose can lead to coma or death. Chronic abuse creates havoc in every system of the body, slowly deteriorating the organs that work overtime to try and metabolize the poison ingested into the body. The effects of acute intoxication are well-known and somewhat easy to recognize: slurred speech, unsteady gait, perceptual distortions, mood changes, and a host of other symptoms that are specific to each individual.

## Marijuana

The second most frequently used substance is marijuana, favored by well over half of high school seniors who admit to having tried it at least once. Although marijuana is not a narcotic and does not cause physiological dependence, it can lead to habitual use because of the euphoric and relaxing feelings it produces. It may be used as an artificial crutch with which students "self-medicate" their stress and personal discomfort rather than face their problems. Finally, it may also be a transitional drug in which the user "graduates" to even more powerful substances.

Marijuana intoxication is often difficult to detect as its effects are rather subtle. There is, of course, the distinctive odor that can be sensed on a child's clothing. Oftentimes, behavior may be socially inappropriate—uncontrollable giggling, unusual facial expressions, withdrawal. In addition, the eyes may appear glassy and dilated, and the person may appear lethargic and tired. A student who is determined to mask the fact that he or she is intoxicated can probably do so without the most expert observer noticing.

Although at one time marijuana was viewed as a relatively harmless recreational drug because it is considered a mild intoxicant and is not physically addictive, thinking has changed considerably in the last decade. We now recognize that marijuana and related substances (hashish, PCP) are extremely habit-forming. Chronic use can lead to decreased motivation, even indifference to events in daily life. Academic achievement, social adjustment, and physical and emotional development are all negatively impacted by marijuana and other hallucinogenic drugs (LSD, mescaline, peyote, psilocybin).

### Stimulants (Cocaine)

Stimulants, including cocaine, rank third in frequency of use by students. These drugs speed up the central nervous system, increase heart rate, depress appetite, and decrease fatigue. Although, strictly speaking, cocaine belongs in a category by itself, it does create effects similar to drugs we know as "speed," such as amphetamines that are prescribed for weight loss or depression. All of these drugs produce a feeling of euphoria, and, although not necessarily physically addictive, they create strong psychological cravings because of rapid onset of the "rush."

In mild forms, nicotine and caffeine are both examples of socially acceptable forms of speed that are quite common. A person who drinks several cups of coffee, for example, will experience many of the symptoms that occur with stronger doses found in "uppers"—increased heart rate, elation and decreased fatigue, higher energy and lower appetite. In addition, sleep is disturbed, anxiety levels are higher, and the person may appear restless, irritable, overtalkative, and agitated. Attention span and comprehension are definitely impaired, so schoolwork is going to suffer.

### Tranquilizers (Depressants)

Tranquilizers are the fourth most commonly used substances by students, and like their chemical cousin, alcohol, these substances are among the most physically addictive drugs. Tranquilizers are also among the most commonly prescribed medications by physicians. In fact, if you were to look in your own medicine cabinet right now, there is a high probability that you have a bottle of Valium® or Xanex® sitting on the shelf. As we mentioned previously, alcohol is another example of a tranquilizer that is often self-prescribed to treat symptoms of stress.

These drugs fall into several categories: minor tranquilizers that are used as mild sedatives to aid sleep or relaxation (Valium®, Xanex®), barbiturates that are used as sleeping pills (Seconal®, Nembutal®), and major tranquilizers that are used to treat psychotic behavior (Thorazine®, Prolixin®). All of these drugs are called "downers" because of the effects they have on the nervous system. They are all highly likely to be addictive, to produce withdrawal symptoms if the person tries to stop, and they are easy to overdose with. In many cases, a person cannot safely get off the drugs without medical supervision.

### Narcotics

Narcotics, also referred to as opiates, are used less often by students than other drugs. They include substances such as morphine (pain suppressant), heroin (recreational drug), codeine (cough suppressant), and Demerol® (muscle relaxant).

Narcotics are highly addictive, and their ability to quickly and effectively reduce pain, appetite, depression, and anxiety increase the likelihood of continued use after initial experimentation. Narcotics are the hardest of the hard drugs, among the most addictive and the most dangerous. Even though the prevalence of their use is considerably less than others you will encounter on a daily basis, especially marijuana and alcohol, they have the most dramatic impact on a child's behavior. You will not see these children for very long; soon after they begin their drug journeys, they will drop out of school in order to support their habits.

## Pay Attention

With these and the other drugs we have mentioned thus far, it is not the acute intoxication that will get your attention in the classroom. Rather, it is the more insidious effects of habitual use or chronic abuse that will affect a child's academic performance, social adjustment, emotional development, and moods and behavior. These children are crying out to you for help, but in a language that you must learn to recognize.

# 3

# Crazy Making: How Addiction Affects the Classroom

The question is not whether your classroom is profoundly under the influence of addictions, but to what extent. Your students' academic performance as well as their social adjustment and emotional well-being are affected by a myriad of factors, probably the least of which is what you have on your lesson plans. Children's psychological and physical health are influenced by what goes on in their homes, their neighborhoods, their bodies, and their peer groups.

As you look around the room at the faces staring up at you, consider how many of them are having their education, their very childhood, compromised by chemical substances. If you are facing a group of adolescents, there is an excellent chance that almost half of them are being affected in their minds and bodies by substances they are taking directly, chemicals that are affecting their abilities to concentrate, their motivation, and their moods and development. Even if you are facing a group of first graders, consider how many of them are negatively affected by addictions in their families and neighborhoods. Then look around your school and reflect on the likelihood that many of your colleagues and peers are struggling with addictive behaviors of their own.

## It Is a Plague on Us

Whether or not you choose to deal firsthand with the problems of the larger society, they inevitably touch your school classroom in many ways. Poverty, gang violence, teenage pregnancy, and the dissolution of the family all have an impact on your effectiveness in reaching students at both personal and academic levels (Kozol, 1991; Towers, 1989). In our work with teachers and counselors, we frequently hear complaints that reflect these larger societal problems that have reached plague-like proportions.

If a plague is an uncontrolled spread of a virulent disease, then certainly what is going on in our classrooms qualifies for that description. Addictions very clearly permeate every corner of our society and make no distinction among race, class, or gender. Whether you teach in a rural or urban area, a large or small building, or a private or public institution; use an elementary or secondary curriculum; or teach an elite or impoverished population, addiction affects what is going on in your classroom, both directly and indirectly.

The addictive and compulsive behaviors of parents, whether with drugs, alcohol, work, or food, profoundly affect the way your students think about themselves and what they do with their lives. Students who come to school depressed, anxious, or angry because of their addicted parents' erratic behavior are not all that interested in what you think might be important. Because they feel distracted, bored, helpless, and frustrated, many see no reason why they should not concentrate their formidable talents and energy on doing whatever they can to disrupt the educational experiences of everyone else. By gosh, they might not be able to fight back against their parents or hostile environment, but you and your classroom sure make attractive targets.

No less profound is the way students who themselves are addicts bring their unpredictable and problematic behaviors to bear on your learning environment. No matter how hard you try to manage your classroom in the face of this addiction phenomenon, unless you address the problems directly, this plague will only grow more infectious.

## Students Who Live Around Addicts

Who are students of addicts? What is their lifestyle? How do they feel about themselves? Where do they go when life at home becomes unbearable? How do these young persons, as students, really affect your classroom? If you haven't personally lived with or around addiction, then these questions may seem odd and only remotely related to classroom teaching. On the other hand, if you have personal experience with this subject, the answers to these questions are abundantly clear. Regardless of whether you know firsthand about addiction, or whether you are trying to get an inside view of it through books like this, the fact remains that unless you develop certain helping skills, the addiction plague will continue to grow.

Students of addicts are children and adolescents of any age living with a parent or guardian who is out of control with a substance, such as alcohol or cocaine, or who is out of control with an extreme lifestyle, such as excessive work habits or aberrant sexual behavior. In these instances, the home environment is centered on the addiction, and life is governed by the addict so that the addictive behavior and all it entails is protected.

Sarah is one of many such examples whose home environment is ruled by addiction. Sarah's father is a weekend alcoholic; when he drinks, he becomes aggressive and violent. As a 12-year-old girl, with a 6-year-old brother and a 4-year-old sister, Sarah is exposed to more abuse than any child should ever have to face.

Sarah knows that her parents will fight on the weekends; it is as much a certainty that her mother will end up battered when it is over. Living in such a battleground, Sarah never brings friends home on the weekends. Rarely is she permitted to visit anyone else.

Sarah secretly believes that if she works hard enough and does everything perfectly, her father will stop drinking and her family will be all right. Sarah's learned perfectionism, and her secret desire to make everything all right at home, have led her to do exceptionally well in school. This does not come easily for her as she has to work twice as hard as her peers to make high scores on class assignments, tests, and report cards. At school, Sarah always does everything that is required and then asks for extra credit assignments to keep her grades high.

All of Sarah's teachers like her and think she is an excellent student. Sarah is cooperative, does not cause trouble in class, and volunteers for all kinds of school and classroom activities. Consequently, Sarah is praised by her teachers, not only for her high performance but for her self-sufficiency; rarely does she ask for help. If they have noticed one area of concern in Sarah's behavior, it is that she has unrealistically high expectations for herself, many that neither she nor anyone could ever reach. Thus, she sets herself up for disappointment and failure because she focuses mostly on her small errors rather than her substantial productivity. Having come from similar environments, this is all too familiar to us as well: We recognize very easily our own tendencies to flagellate ourselves for failing to meet our absurdly high levels of expectation.

To Sarah's teachers, who equate her achievement and compliance with healthy adjustment and who assume her critical emotional needs are being met at home because of her academic success at school, she appears exemplary in almost every way. None of her teachers suspect that when Sarah goes home from school each day, most especially on Fridays, she reenters the controlled world of an alcoholic where she has learned to survive by becoming on overachieving perfectionist.

## Characteristics of Students From Addicted Homes

This case study of Sarah reveals some of the characteristics of children who live with addicts. Although Sarah has been abused at home by her father, at school she appears to be the perfect student. She strives for perfection in all her work and consequently receives approval from teachers. Although Sarah's perfectionist tendencies typify one type of reaction to living with an addicted parent, students can and do react in other ways. For example, some students become rebellious and act out, whereas others become quiet and withdrawn.

*Perfectionism.* Like Sarah, some children living with addicts strive to be perfect in every way. In order to save themselves and their families from embarrassment and to try to hide their family secret of addiction, everything they do must be done right. Being perfect in school means getting high grades and aligning obediently with school rules and regulations. Because high grades do not always come easily for these persons, especially when life at home is often erratic and unpredictable, they learn how to utilize spare moments at school to work on papers until they are free of errors, thus setting up a pattern of compulsive work habits that later in life can develop into workaholism and obsessive perfectionism.

*Fear of failure.* Some students living with addicts also demonstrate a fear of failure. These young persons feel that they are to blame for their parents' addiction and that they have failed as children. If only they were brighter, more cooperative, better looking, less of a disappointment, then their parents would not fight so much. Not wanting to let their parents down, they try harder and harder to do everything to please them, knowing that whatever they do, it will not be enough. This same unhealthy behavior is evident in the classroom as well, much to the delight of teachers who appreciate the high level of involvement without knowing the dear price that is being paid.

*Approval seeking.* Because addicts are focused almost exclusively on self and on maintaining the addiction, family members become a means to this end. That is, children are used in many ways by the addict to keep the addiction alive. Additionally, addicts are often in an altered state of consciousness. Their decision-making capacities are impaired. They have perceptual and cognitive deficits. Their moods are erratic and violent. They have a number of health problems, financial difficulties, and interpersonal struggles. They are not exactly model parents.

Students in these home environments, then, may constantly seek the approval and affirmation from teachers and friends at school that they don't get at home. These students are seeking reassurance from teachers as the only adults who can validate them. Such students are often found lingering by your desk, hanging on to your every gesture and word, waiting for some endorsement by you that they are still in your good graces. They will not risk thinking for themselves or doing anything that might jeopardize your favorable impression.

*Abusive relationships.* Relationships tend to be abusive in homes where one or both parents are addicts. Although children living within these environments live in constant fear of the abusive parent, they nonetheless become habituated to the torture. These children tend to have increased levels of fear and anxiety, they experience low self-esteem, and years of living with an addicted parent or guardian leads them to develop relationship patterns that are dysfunctional. They have learned not to expect much from others.

In addition to habituated relationship patterns, students who live with an addicted parent may also feel they have been abandoned by their parent(s), and indeed this is so. Addicted parents may be gone for long periods of time, either bingeing on their addiction or recovering from it. And even when an addicted parent does not leave home, there may be periods of time when the parent is so utterly consumed by the addiction that the child is essentially alone. Fear of abandonment, coupled with low self-esteem, may cause students to develop relationships that are filled with extreme jealousy. This form of behavior, although inappropriate, safeguards the child of an addict from fear of abandonment and ensures love that is often explicitly lacking at home.

*Low self-esteem.* A common trait of students who live with an addicted parent is low self-esteem. At home they are unable to develop a sense of individual identity; rather, they are inclined to build the identity and esteem of the addicted parent. Adolescents, who have a deep need to develop a sense of personal autonomy, are unable to master this crucial developmental task. Because they don't have their esteem needs met at home, they seek to build this in other settings. This is done in different ways, including becoming a perfectionist, acting out and getting into trouble, or entering into relationships where their self-esteem depends on their partner.

*Mood swings.* An addicted person is unpredictable, showing rage and anger one day, then docility and kindness the next. Consider, for example, a child who witnesses a drunken father beating his wife one day, then hugging her affectionately and apologetically the next morning. Additionally, moods for the addicted parent may show weekly changes that align with the drinking pattern, ranging from very bad moods early in the week as the result of a drunken weekend to more jovial moods toward the end of the week in anticipation of more indulgence.

Mood swings are common for students whose addicted parents show similar trends. Like their addicted parents, students' mood swings in the classroom can vary, according to Towers (1989), "from rage to depression, with everything in between, such as anger, anxiety, interest, calm, relaxation, disinterest, or boredom" (p. 20). Mood swings can also come from the love-hate relationships that students have with family, partly because of the moods of the addicted parent. A young person may love his or her addicted father or mother as a parent but hate who they are as an addict, thus leading to a love-hate relationship and causing ambivalent feelings. Because the child is dependent on the family for basic needs (e.g., food, shelter, nurturing), mood swings surface as feelings of love one day and hate the next day.

### Students Who Are Addicts

Most teachers know at least several students in their classes who are using drugs regularly. This is especially true for teachers at middle schools and high schools where drug use is an ever-present threat to the emotional stability of students (Walter et al., 1991). Children are more likely to become addicted to a substance when their parents are users or when parents are addicted to an extreme lifestyle (McKay et al., 1992).

As we discussed in the previous chapter, students who become addicted to substances, whether they are emulating a parent or trying to fit into a peer group, demonstrate behaviors that are counterproductive to learning in school classrooms. Not only is their ability to concentrate impaired but they are also likely to influence the behavior of other classmates.

Suzanne was 16 years old when she was referred by her therapist for inpatient drug treatment. She had been having a number of conflicts with her mother that were both the cause and effect of declining grades in school. Since her parents' divorce, Suzanne had been living with her mother, seeing her father about once a month.

When Suzanne first began seeing an outpatient therapist, she had dropped out of the high school chorus and debate clubs. She isolated herself more and more from school-related functions. Her grades dropped from As and Bs to Cs and Ds. She stated that school was a stupid waste of time and she had a hostile attitude toward teachers. Suzanne did voice an interest in going to college, however.

Suzanne began drinking alcohol at the age of 14. It began innocently enough, sipping beer with a few friends. Next, she experimented with smoking marijuana. Suzanne drank alcohol and used marijuana primarily on weekends, about two to three times per month throughout her freshman year in high school. During the summer following her freshman year, she also began experimenting with LSD, as well as increasing the frequency of smoking pot and drinking.

During her sophomore year, Suzanne tried to control her drug and alcohol use because she didn't want it to interfere with schoolwork. Nevertheless, she continued to use heavily on weekends and began breaking curfew at home so she could party with her friends. It was at this time that she started dating a guy who was known to be kind of wild. Suzanne's friends, who she had known since junior high school, didn't like her new boyfriend much and became concerned about her alcohol and drug use. She became more isolated from friends and began to withdraw from school activities.

During the summer after her sophomore year, her substance use escalated to abusive levels. She became more involved with a drug-using subculture. At times, she would even sell drugs for her boyfriend. Suzanne experienced several alcohol-induced blackouts that summer. Her tolerance increased, she began using alone, and she began using early in the day. Suzanne also tried cocaine several times that summer.

As she began her junior year in high school, her level of substance indulgence continued to increase. She smoked pot before school and even between classes. She frequently missed school because she stayed out too late the night before. Suzanne also began shoplifting with drug-using friends and stole money from her mother's purse. At the time Suzanne was admitted for inpatient treatment, she was addicted to alcohol and marijuana.

### Characteristics of Addicted Students

This case study of Suzanne reveals some of the characteristics of children who become addicted to substances in their adolescent years. This story also points to how school for these students takes on secondary importance as addiction becomes central to their lives. Through Suzanne's experience, we can see gradual apathy toward school, unpredictable behavior, absenteeism, and eventually theft. Less obvious in this case, although assuredly present for Suzanne and others like her, are fatigue and listlessness, memory and concentration problems with schoolwork, and retarded emotional development.

*Tardiness and absenteeism.* In the early phases of substance use, when students begin experimenting with substances at school, tardiness and absenteeism may not be problems. As students begin using more often, as Suzanne did, then tardiness is likely to increase.

When use of substances becomes the central organizing factor in students' lives and when they have entered into a subculture that is organized around drug and alcohol use, school becomes something less than a priority. Even the purpose of school changes from a place where social and academic development are foremost to a place where drug deals are consummated. Skipping classes is a common phenomenon as drug-using students seek to get high and stay that way throughout the day. When they are in class, these students tend to be apathetic and listless.

*Erratic and unpredictable behavior*. Addicted students, when they come to class, are often temperamental in the ways they respond to teachers and their peers. They can be withdrawn one moment, explosive the next. They can appear completely indifferent to what is going on around them, and then so overinvolved that they react in ways that are out of proportion to what might be expected. When under the influence, these students can be passive, almost calm, and cause no trouble at all. Although they might not be learning all that you had hoped, they at least are not causing trouble for others. On other days, however, when students are not high but are anticipating a drug purchase or waiting for friends between classes to get high, these students can be nervous, highly excitable, and anxious. Students who are into heavy use are more concerned with their addiction than with your class, and they simply don't care if they cause trouble. Indeed, some would like to be kicked out of your class to have a legitimate reason to be out of school.

*Underachievement and memory defects*. When students are preoccupied with using drugs or booze, and when substance abuse has become central to their life, it is not surprising that these students fail to reach their academic potential. Some substance-using students are very bright, and involvement with drugs and its accompanying culture lead them to leave behind their schoolwork as they assimilate drugs into their lives. Their intellectual potential and any contributions they could make to the school and to their peers in school clubs is lost.

Some drugs, such as LSD, may cause students to have memory lapses. And heavy abuse of alcohol causes blackouts, or lack of ability to remember periods of time while under the influence. In these instances, schoolwork can be drastically impaired. In fact, when we consider the rapid rate at which children's minds and bodies are growing, ingesting any chemical into their systems is likely to have deleterious effects.

*Crime and gangs*. Involvement in crime, such as theft and shoplifting, is a natural consequence of substance abuse. Students who use drugs regularly steal money from family members in order to support their expensive habits. And heavy users sell drugs to peers at school to support their use. Even a moderate crack cocaine habit is likely to cost thousands of dollars, far more than what an adolescent can obtain from allowance or part-time jobs.

Street gangs are often centered on substance use and addiction. Although the cultural and sociological dimensions of gangs are complex and are beyond the scope of our discussion here, we want to emphasize that when students have a change in peer groups, as Suzanne did, and when the change involves association with gang members, drug use is likely, if not inevitable.

*Fatigue and listlessness.* Student addicts, in many ways, are no different than adult addicts. They spend their waking hours thinking about how to keep their addiction alive. When they are in your class, staring blankly at their books, they are thinking about what awaits them when the bell rings. When they are out of school, they spend time with friends who are also hooked into an addictive lifestyle.

As we have mentioned, in the later stages of addiction, students begin using substances when they are alone. While at home, students might have to hide their use from parents and siblings, staying up late at night to get high or sneaking out to be with friends and breaking curfew at home. Consequently, they might exhibit sleepiness in class.

## Teachers Have Addictions of Their Own

Teachers provide young children, early adolescents, and high school teenagers with powerful role models. This is a weighty responsibility because we are always in the spotlight. Students know how we are feeling; they sense our moods as easily as meteorologists observe the weather. They immediately notice when we are wearing our hair a bit differently or when we are wearing a new outfit. They watch our every move. After all, we are their keepers.

Because teachers are always "on stage" as role models for students, we are expected to project good habits and ethically correct behavior. Even parents can be flawed, but we are supposed to be paid professionals who live up to a higher standard of goodness. Yet we are human too. We have our problems and needs. We live with stress and conflict. We feel overburdened and overworked. We do all that we can to hold our lives together. Sometimes inadvertently, or because we have no other choice (so it feels), we engage in addictive habits of our own that are visible to anyone who cares to notice.

## Legal Addiction

We are sensitive to the fact that even by including this discussion we may provoke defensiveness, even outrage, in some readers. How dare we suggest that teachers are part of the problem in creating classrooms under the influence!

Yet what message do we communicate to students when they smell smoke on the clothes of a teacher, knowing that he or she has just been indulging in a tobacco addiction? Why are students not allowed the same privilege (and it very much seems like a privilege because teachers can do it but students cannot)? What do they make of the situation when they see us consume coffee, tea, or cola beverages for fortification during the middle of the day? How do they interpret the need for those "nerve pills" lying on the teacher's desk? How do they interpret our daily doses of donuts or candy for a "sugar high"? What do students think when they see us stumble in on Monday morning, recovering from a hung-over weekend?

An important issue surrounding the use of licit drugs is their effect on the moods and energy levels of teachers and consequently on the atmosphere of the classroom. Like students who are energetic, talkative, or more difficult to manage just after lunch, teachers too have energy and mood swings throughout the day. We all have daily rhythms that we follow. For licit drug users, these rhythms are exacerbated. Questions that surface from licit drug use include, How energetic and jovial is a coffee-addicted teacher in the classroom when there is no morning cup of coffee? and How nervous and agitated is the teacher who is unable to go to the lounge for an expected smoke between classes? Clearly, some classroom learning environments are powerfully affected by the licit drug use of teachers. Moreover, when teachers bring their addictions into the classroom, regardless of how harmless these habits might appear, they send messages to their students about living a life governed by chemical substances. Do these messages, in some way, give students a license to use drugs of their own?

## Illicit Addiction and Extreme Lifestyles

Although teachers are expected to maintain high standards for themselves and their profession at school, they too become addicted to illicit substances. We assume that this encompasses a very small percentage of the teaching force, but we also realize that addiction is a very real phenomenon for teachers. Although it is unlikely that a teacher who has been having problems in this area would be reading this book (preferring to hide in denial), it is probable that you know of at least one colleague who is struggling with an addiction. Perhaps it is someone undergoing a divorce who is "medicating" him- or herself with booze to get through the transition or someone you know who uses food to feed fragile self-esteem. It could be a colleague who has been taking tranquilizers for some time in order to cope with nerves or even someone who has been prescribed diet or sleeping pills on a regular basis. Most likely of all, you may know other teachers whose recreational use of alcohol and other drugs has gotten out of hand.

All of this information is, of course, quite underground. The consequences for a teacher of being discovered to have a drug problem are quite severe. Whether we choose to acknowledge this as a crisis or not, there is no reason to believe that teachers should be any more exempt than other professionals in their susceptibility to addiction. When we consider how high the burnout and stress levels are in schools, we have reason to believe that teachers might even be as vulnerable as emergency-room physicians.

## Teachers Who Live (or Have Lived) With an Addict

Like students who live with addicted parents, teachers too may come from addicted households. The ways a teacher functions, the patience he or she shows on a given day, and the attitudes and moods displayed in class are all influenced by what has happened at home the day before. A teacher who has been living with an alcoholic for years is likely to show symptoms of codependency, as well as other dysfunctional enabling behaviors. A teacher whose own child is an addict is likely to be something less than objective on the subject. This teacher may very well be carrying around a tremendous burden of guilt that will affect interactions with other children. Similarly, the teacher with an addicted parent or sibling will have played a role in maintaining that behavior and will also have a history of frustration in trying to be helpful. All of these personal experiences will influence what happens in the classroom.

Elsewhere, two of us (Powell & Zehm, 1991) reported the case study of Bill, a student teacher who was the child of an alcoholic. We discovered from interviews with Bill and from observations of his classroom teaching that his inability to manage the classroom and effectively discipline students was a consequence of being raised in an alcoholic home. The trouble that Bill had with student discipline is described briefly below.

Bill, a middle-aged student teacher, entered the teaching profession later in life, as a second career. Bill's cooperating teacher, Mr. Allen, observed that Bill had trouble managing his classroom. His lesson planning and record keeping were described as "compulsively fastidious" and "exemplary," but his ability to maintain a classroom environment conducive to learning was observed as "entirely lacking." Bill's lack of classroom control and effective management persisted to the very end of student teaching, even with exemplary mentoring.

Mr. Allen described Bill as nonassertive, lacking in the initiative it takes to keep children on task. Students in Bill's classes would persistently interrupt the lesson, walk around the room, sleep uninterrupted during class, and talk to their peers during the lessons.

Bill would teach only to those students who paid attention to him. Rarely was he observed correcting students or enforcing discipline. Even in these instances, Bill failed to carry out the threats and ultimatums.

During several private conferences, Bill revealed that he was raised in a "difficult alcoholic home" and had not been involved in any type of personal recovery program. When asked about his apparent inability to control his students, to get students on task, and to demand their attention, he noted,

> I am afraid to ask students to pay attention and act right. I would rather do anything than get into an argument with a student. I feel afraid and anxious when I get into arguments with them. It's the same feeling I had when my dad and mom fought all those times that Dad came home drunk. (Powell & Zehm, 1991, p. 10)

Many teachers, especially beginners, have difficulty with classroom management and student discipline. Indeed, this is a foremost concern for all student teachers (Veenam, 1984). Bill's case nonetheless illuminates how a teacher whose parent was addicted to alcohol may negatively influence the classroom learning environment. Bill's example also points to the importance for all educators to become aware of the ways that living with an addicted person influences the classroom learning environment.

## The Addicted Classroom Environment

Our purpose with this chapter was to consider how the addiction phenomenon influences the classroom learning environment. By focusing on children living with addicted parents, on children who are themselves addicts or who are becoming addicted, and on teachers who are, in various ways, addicted to licit and illicit substances, we have highlighted how classrooms can become environments controlled by addictions.

The three stories we have presented to you in this chapter (i.e., Sarah, Suzanne, and Bill) reveal how addiction influences your classroom. The example of Sarah also shows how subtle and deceiving the influence can be, especially because the school rewards student behavior like that shown by her. However, in rewarding Sarah with attention and good grades, the likelihood of her becoming an overachiever later in life, coupled with compulsive work habits and obsessive perfectionism, is increased. On the other hand, schools tend to be unforgiving to persons like Suzanne who have trouble coping with the structure of school in the face of their addiction. Teachers like Bill get bad evaluations from their administrators, and students' off-task behavior is increased in these classrooms. Indeed, because of the negative evaluations Bill received from his supervising teacher during student teaching, he was unable to get a teaching job.

Clearly, addiction does influence the classroom in profound ways. But how, in the face of this addiction phenomenon, does the school deal with this social malady? In the previous examples, the school rewards the dysfunctional behavior of Sarah, punishes the dysfunctional behavior of Suzanne, and pushes potentially good teachers like Bill out of the classroom. In each of these cases and in several others we will follow in the next chapters, there are special challenges for teachers for which we have been wholly unprepared.

# 4

# So Many Places to Hide:
# The Special Challenges for Teachers

In the preceding chapters, we established that children of addicts live in chaotic environments. These children are highly anxious and often suffer from stress-related problems such as stomachaches, headaches, sleep disorders, and a host of emotional problems. Although children from addictive environments may also be experiencing severe depression, they are also quite good at masking their symptoms: They have found so many places to hide their fear, insecurity, and anger. All you may see sitting in your classroom is a student who appears a bit sullen and withdrawn. Perhaps, you wonder, he or she is just a bit shy.

You can easily identify some students who are more extreme in their acting-out behaviors. The vast majority, however, are overlooked if they do not draw attention to themselves in dramatic ways. Another problem is that some teachers are unfamiliar with the signs and symptoms of addiction and other emotional disorders as they are manifested in the classroom (Kottler & Kottler, 1993). You notice that a child overreacts when you reach out to give a reassuring touch, that he or she appears reluctant to go home after school, that he or she has complained of nightmares, but it does not occur to you that he or she may be sexually abused. Other children may show signs of depression, anxiety, eating disorders, or phobic or conduct disorders, but unless you know what to look for, all you will see is a child who is acting strangely.

As a classroom teacher, you are in a vitally important position to help these students; perhaps nobody is in a better position. They might not trust their parents. They don't know the school counselor very well. Their friends are fine, but they crave an adult perspective on what is going on. You see them on a daily basis. They trust you. If you have done your job, then you have created relationships with many of your students in which they feel accepted and respected. They know that you are someone they can reach out to.

### Through Children's Eyes

Helping children from addictive environments requires that you first appropriately identify them and learn about their culture and, second, that you accurately diagnose their needs. Identification and diagnosis are two of the special challenges in teaching these students. We do not want to imply, however, that these students need to be part of a pullout program, nor should they be placed with a special group of students. This is exactly what should not happen, because the labeling that goes along with these programs would serve to further undermine these students' fragile self-concept.

Examining the special challenges involved when working with children of addicts requires you to adapt, if not restructure, the way you operate your classroom. This will be even more of a challenge if you have been teaching for several years—your routines and expectations are well established. If you have not been particularly aware that your classroom has been functioning under the influence of addictions, then you may not even see much point in changing something you believe has already been working fairly well.

To see some of these invisible effects, you will have to abandon reliance solely on your own perceptions so that you can see through the eyes of your students. This is the essence of what is meant by true empathy, the willingness to suspend your own preconceptions and internal frame of reference in favor of the perspective of those whom, you serve. This means entering each child's world, not only as a tourist who is looking around but as a participant, as one who not only can sense what the child is feeling but actually think and feel just as the child does.

People often wonder how it is possible that therapists can appear to read minds, anticipate what people will do next, and even predict the future. If the truth be known, there is no magic or wizardry involved; it is simply a matter of accurate empathy, immersing oneself completely into the world of the other. With respect to the children of addicts or substance abusers themselves, this means accessing their feelings of inadequacy, the rage and fear that they mask, and the sense of helplessness and being out of control. When you can move beyond imagining how they must feel and really feel their pain and hurt in your heart, that is when you will read their minds and make sense of behavior that had previously seemed incomprehensible.

For all of the special challenges we review in this chapter, it is empathy that will test you the most. On the one hand, you are trying to get inside these children's worlds, to resonate with their deepest stirrings, to see the world through their eyes. Yet on the other hand, you must set boundaries so that you don't lose yourself in the process, so that you don't permit their pain to become your pain. Of equal importance is not allowing yourself to feel such sympathy for them that you are unable to enforce the rules and limits that they so crave. The paradox in working with those who have addiction problems is that they require both a deep level of empathic sensitivity and also a very firm hand to stop all attempts at manipulation, control, acting out, and approval seeking. That is the ultimate challenge for teachers.

We have identified five major challenges that teachers face in their interactions with children under the influence of addiction. Naturally, there are far more than a mere handful, but these are representative of the subtle and complex ways in which the addiction phenomenon affects classroom functioning. First, we consider the challenge you have in recognizing the denial that surrounds and protects addiction. Then we discuss diagnosis of students and their needs. The third challenge we discuss is how to approach students. Fourth, we consider the challenge you have in recognizing the destructive urges these students exhibit. Finally, we discuss escape fantasies that many of these students adopt.

## The First Challenge: Recognizing Denial

If you are successful in your attempts to adopt an empathic posture and enter the child's world, it is likely you would say to yourself, "I feel afraid of this class and especially this teacher who pretends to care about me. I know she can't really care all that much because I am not worth loving. Adults have betrayed me in the past; this teacher is no different. In fact, she is more dangerous to me than most because I can feel myself trusting her. I've got to stop her from getting too close, from finding out my secret. I want to escape, to hide, to make this nightmare go away. Since I can't leave this class, I have to find some way to keep things under control, on my own terms. If I make myself as unlovable as possible, cause problems, stir things up, then maybe she will leave me alone."

Of course, rarely are such conscious thoughts so explicit. The nature of denial, as a defense mechanism, is that it permits the child to ward off many of these threatening feelings and realizations. The actual dialogue that would take place inside the child's head, once denial has kicked in gear, is more likely to resemble, "The creep is always on my case. I don't have a problem. Why doesn't he just get off my back? Everything is cool. No problem. I've got things under control."

Empathy helps you to decode behavior that previously has seemed bizarre and irrational. Denial is a powerful device because it works so well. When children cannot deal with things that are too overwhelming, denial allows them to put it out of sight, almost out of mind. The same is true for this device as it operates in other arenas.

*Classroom challenge: to help students overcome behaviors that perpetuate denial of addiction in themselves or their family and denial of their feelings.*

Denial is the phenomenon whereby students avoid openly and honestly talking about addiction, especially if their parents are using substances like alcohol or drugs, or when a parent becomes habituated to extreme lifestyles such as compulsive sex or excessive gambling. In these homes, the addiction is central to life. The addict will not allow anyone to criticize the habit, and because of the compulsive and obsessive nature of this lifestyle, the addict protects the habit by oppressing family members.

This denial process for students usually means developing behaviors that cover up the addiction. The challenge for you as a teacher is, first of all, to be aware that denial exists. By definition, attempts are made to deceive, disguise, and otherwise hide the secret. This challenge is further complicated by variations in denial behaviors that students exhibit. For example, these behaviors might include extreme acting out, complete withdrawal, becoming a class clown, or turning into an overachieving "teacher pleaser" (Black, 1979; Deutsch, 1982; Powell, Gabe, & Zehm, 1994).

*Classroom challenge: to confront and begin overcoming your own denial of the addiction phenomenon.*

Like your students, you might also be deceiving yourself. In denial, you choose not to deal with addiction and you argue that it has no real influence on your teaching. Moreover, if you are living with someone who is an addict or if you spent much of your life being raised by an addict, you may also pretend that these factors are not relevant to what you do in the classroom. You are hoping that nobody will notice or, better yet, that the problems will resolve themselves. This almost never happens.

*Classroom challenge: for professional school staff—including teachers, administrators, and counselors—to increase awareness of and sensitivity toward addiction; to learn ways for dealing with the addiction phenomenon in school classrooms.*

There are issues facing schools today that only a few decades ago did not exist. The rise in non-English-speaking and limited-English-proficient students and cultural diversity, for example, have created exciting new challenges for schools. On the other hand, substance abuse, street gang tension, and culturally insensitive curricula are interfering with the learning process. Yet the malady of addiction, and how it influences children at school, has received relatively little attention. Perhaps this is because schools in general feel that problems at home are best left at home and that there are already enough problems to deal with without entering into the realm of addiction too. Yet addiction at home underlies many of the other types of problems that schools face. Absenteeism, tardiness, discipline referrals, student apathy, substance abuse, and child abuse have all been directly linked to the addiction phenomenon at home. However, schools choose to remain in denial of addiction, thinking that if they look the other way long enough then perhaps the problem will take care of itself. In the meantime, addiction is taking hold of school classrooms in subtle yet powerful ways.

*Classroom challenge: to understand how societal denial is part of your personal denial as well as part of students' denial of their own and their parents' addictions.*

Certainly, on a larger scale, society has ways of remaining in denial of addiction. This includes a disowning of both substance addiction and lifestyle addiction. Persons addicted to exercise and running, for example, may be viewed by society as staying fit and healthy. As another example, parents who are addicted to work, spending almost every waking moment on task with work-related duties, might be viewed as making an honest living, working hard to pay bills and get ahead financially. However, these societal views serve to reinforce addictive behaviors related to extreme lifestyles.

These workaholic behaviors are even modeled at the highest levels. During a recent presidential administration, hordes of young, ambitious, talented top-level staff members burned out after a single year in office. The cultural environment of their work setting, with a sterling example set by the president himself, was that there was no limit to how many hours you should devote to your job on behalf of your country. Working 70, 80, 90 hours per week had become the norm. Family contact, recreational activities, leisure pursuits, even eating and sleeping were put on hold in favor of the drive to work harder, work more hours, and show others how devoted you really were.

Most societal views of addiction tend to be limited to substance abuse. As we noted above, however, many of our students live with mothers and fathers who are addicted to their work, obsessed with religion, or consumed by exercise or diet. Children living in homes governed by lifestyle addictions (as opposed to chemical addictions) experience the same feelings of rejection, loss of love, and lack of predictable home environment. When society condones excessive lifestyles and when it fails to openly and honestly address addiction at home, it implicitly supports excessive and addictive habits.

Denial, then, is a pervasive and complicated phenomenon that all of us deal with on a daily basis. As teachers, your challenge is to understand how these forms of denial are influencing the students you teach every day. You are, therefore, in an ideal position to

- Help alter behavior patterns that perpetuate students' denial
- Work toward overcoming your own denial
- Discuss school denial with counselors, administrators, and other teachers
- Recognize the forms of societal denial that affect what you do in your classroom
- Acknowledge and confront denial in the life of your classroom

### The Second Challenge: Making Accurate Diagnoses

Once you understand how denial fosters addiction in your classroom, you can more effectively diagnose children living within addictive environments and then determine how to more directly meet their needs. The application of this assessment process means not only being able to recognize the children who are obviously troubled (acting out, withdrawn, etc.) but also those who are manifesting more subtle symptoms (approval seeking, perfectionistic tendencies, etc.). In general, assessment at any level involves asking yourself a series of internal questions:

- What is distinctive or unusual about this child's behavior?
- Has there been a noticeable change of behavior?
- In what ways may this child be crying out for help?
- Is there evidence of some underlying emotional disorder?
- What are the signs and symptoms of acute depression and anxiety?
- What do I know about the student's home environment that might shed light on the problem?
- What more do I need to know? How can I find out?
- What specific symptoms is the child showing? Memory deficits? Irresponsibility? Flight of ideas? Mood alterations? Thought disorders? Change in appearance?

In addition, the formal diagnosis of drug dependence is characterized by at least three of nine symptoms that include (American Psychiatric Association, 1994) the following: (a) substance taken in larger doses over a period of time; (b) a persistent desire for the substance; (c) lots of time spent trying to obtain the substance and recover from its effects; (d) frequent intoxication that interferes with work or school responsibilities; (e) normal extracurricular or leisure activities abandoned because of substance abuse; (f) continued use even after realizing there has been some physical, emotional, family, or social deterioration; (g) need for greater doses of substance in order to get high (tolerance); (h) withdrawal symptoms; and (i) substance needed to avoid withdrawal symptoms.

This is, of course, the most basic line of inquiry. There are actually quite a few tests that can be administered by counselors and psychologists to determine whether there is actually a treatable problem. Some of these tests involve addiction-severity indexes, whereas others require a physical examination and detailed family history. None of this is going to happen, however, unless you are observant enough to recognize that there might be something going on. You are the professional who will most likely initiate some kind of action.

## The Third Challenge: Approaching Students

*Classroom challenge: to know when and how to approach a student that you suspect is a child of an addict and whom you've identified as needing your special attention.*

It is one thing to think you know what is going on with a student who may be troubled; it is quite another to do something about it. Witness, for example, the following dialogue that is quite typical of what could happen:

*Teacher:* "Karyn, I noticed that you haven't been as perky as usual."

*Student:* "So?"

*Teacher:* "Well, I was wondering if something was going on with you, whether there was something I might do to help?"

*Student* (under her breath): "It's none of your business."

*Teacher:* "Excuse me?"

*Student:* "Nothing. I was just saying that everything is fine. Nothing is wrong." (Student starts to walk away.)

*Teacher:* "Wait, Karyn! Please. I have noticed in the past few months that your grades have been getting steadily worse. You rarely turn in homework, and that is not like you. In class, you stare out the window. You seem lost. I really would like to help if I can."

*Student:* "I appreciate it, I really do. It's just nothing I want to talk about. Can I go now?"

This teacher has done everything exactly as she should have. She was direct. She provided specific feedback on what she has observed. She demonstrated her concern, yet in a way that was neither accusatory or pushy. She did what she could to communicate that she was concerned and interested in being of assistance. Yet still her efforts were rebuffed, at least after this first overture. It may very well transpire that the next day, perhaps a week later, or even a month in the future, Karyn will feel safe enough, or perhaps desperate enough, to approach the one adult in her life whom she can turn to. The key for the teacher is to (a) observe carefully, (b) remain available without being intrusive, and (c) continue using relationship skills to work on trust issues.

Identifying students of addicts and examining their patterns of denial can be done by you alone, or you can recruit the assistance of specialists such as the school psychologist, social worker, or counselor. Before you approach students about addictive problems in their home, first observe them over time and chart their behaviors. In your observations, try to look for trends and key factors that indicate an addictive environment.

In the case of Karyn, her teacher started keeping more detailed records after her first attempt to reach out to her. She thought there might be some time in the future when such systematic data gathering could prove helpful. Over the period of the next few weeks she charted instances of tardiness, homework assignments not turned in, test scores, contributions to class, interactions with peers, and even smiles that were visible. Although this required some effort on the teacher's part, these data proved invaluable in getting the attention of Karyn's parents, as well as help from the school counselor to take this problem seriously.

As far as the way you approach a target student, we suggest being as open, trustful, caring, and nonjudgmental as possible. You must be genuine in your effort to help him or her. Avoid telling students that you think their parents may be abusing alcohol or drugs or that you suspect they are being sexually abused. This up-front approach may intimidate students and force them to retreat behind their shield of denial.

Certain skills favored by counselors are also quite useful by teachers in the classroom (Kottler & Kottler, 1993). Active listening, for example, involves staying away from giving advice, instructing, or otherwise acting like a teacher. Instead, the emphasis is on attending and listening carefully to what the child is saying, reflecting the feelings and content you hear in a nondirective way that communicates that you really do understand:

*Student:* "It's really not so bad at home. I mean, my parents are doing the best they can and all. I don't blame them or anything."

*Teacher:*   "Your heart goes out to your parents. You want to help but you feel so helpless. I also sense that you feel angry at them for disrupting your life but also guilty for feeling this way."

This is just one of a dozen skills that can be learned and practiced in such a way that students feel heard and understood by you. When they feel ready to reach out for help, you are the person they will come to first.

We advise you to approach these students by expressing your genuine concern about their well-being. For the withdrawn child, you might say, "I notice how very quiet you are. I really would like for you to participate more, but I'm not sure how to encourage you to do that. What can I do to help you so that you might feel more comfortable?" This kind of nonjudgmental approach invites students to talk with you in a trustful manner and suggests your sincerity and compassion for their needs. As trust is built between you and students, you can then consider various intervention strategies that are presented in later chapters.

If you don't feel comfortable approaching a particular student directly or you feel the specific problem of addiction is too sensitive for you to handle at school, you can ask a school counselor or other person in charge of students' special needs to help you. Although this approach is less useful in building trust between you and the student, it nevertheless is helpful when you might not have time to talk with the student, or when you feel that a particular school counselor may be better skilled at handling these situations.

### The Fourth Challenge: Recognizing Destructive Urges

Another set of challenges to working with children of addicts in your classroom is identifying and addressing the destructive urges these children develop. This is especially difficult because some of these urges are reinforced and encouraged by the school culture and by society in general, such as overachievement. The children of addicts are often the most favored students by any teacher. We like their obedient, deferential behavior. We are seduced by their tendencies to placate and compliment us. We are appreciative that they are willing to work so hard, often without considering the price they are paying internally.

Because these children do not all have the same life experiences, they don't have identical problems or needs (Tharinger & Koranek, 1988) nor do they have the same destructive urges. Moreover, some students have lived so long in an environment predominated by addiction that their destructive urges, which can also be described as survival strategies, have become habitual. These students may not even know they have these urges until they are helped by you to reflect closely on their own behavior.

Below are destructive urges that debilitate life for children of addicts, both in and out of school. Your challenge in the classroom is to recognize and intervene in these counterproductive patterns of behavior.

### Self-Depreciation

*Classroom challenge: to work toward building self-esteem and confidence for all students, particularly for students from home environments where addiction predominates life.*

Children of addicts tend to put themselves down (Berkowitz & Perkins, 1988). Feeling unloved and unwanted, they have developed low self-esteem, a poor self-image, and little confidence in themselves. What these students need is a safe, trusting classroom environment where they are helped to feel good about themselves. Because many of these students undervalue themselves as students and deprecate themselves as persons, they may attend school irregularly, underachieve on assignments and exams, and eventually drop out of school altogether. Helping these children to overcome their self-deprecating behaviors in your classroom is exceedingly important in enabling them to see themselves as valuable persons who are worthy of your trust and concern.

*Student:*  "I don't know the answer to that one. I just can't do it.
I'm stupid."

*Teacher:*  "What you mean to say is that this is difficult for you.
Whereas sometimes you may *feel* stupid, or even *act*
stupidly, you never *are* stupid. That is an absolute
label you put on yourself. I have seen a number of
instances when you appear to be quite intelligent,
even brilliant in your thinking. That is hardly the
behavior of an individual who is stupid."

### Hyperactivity and Nervous Energy

*Classroom challenge: to help these students redirect their energy
into productive channels; to increase your patience for working with
students of addicts.*

Some children of addicts exhibit hyperactivity; they just
can't sit still. Such a flurry of energy is productive for some of
these students; they are constantly on task doing assignments
and activities, especially those who tend to overachieve. For
other students, however, their unharnessed energy gets them into
trouble. They stand up in the middle of class without permis-
sion, move around in the classroom often indiscriminately, and
shuffle their feet more than their peers. They might not intend
to be a nuisance, but their hyperactivity causes interference in
lessons and gets other students off task. These students then
receive more of your frustration and anger than other students.

### Escape Artists

*Classroom challenge: to help students who are escape artists to
live productively in the reality of your classroom, to know when they
are exhibiting escapist behavior; to assist students in learning more
appropriate ways to exist in the moment.*

Children of addicts, especially those who themselves have
become substance abusers, are experts at escaping their immediate reality. They learned escape strategies at home to survive
their addictive environments, and they take these strategies
everywhere with them, including into your classroom. These
skills might include withdrawal (e.g., the forgotten child), acting out, or being a class clown (see Deutsch, 1982). Another

strategy for some students is to become perfect in all that they do, turning in flawless papers and always searching for extra-credit points. Although you would like to have students who try to be perfect on their papers and who consistently strive for excellence, you assuredly would not like to feel what they are feeling inside and what they have to experience at home.

## Self-Abuse

*Classroom challenge: to recognize and counteract students' self-abusive disorders both in and out of your classroom.*

Children and adolescents who are raised with addiction tend to become self-abusive, although they may be unaware of this phenomenon. That is, the behavior they demonstrate may appear normal for them because they are trying to cope with and accommodate to an unpredictable and threatening home situation.

If a child feels worthless, unentitled to a satisfying, enjoyable, and productive life, he or she may try to duplicate the pain that has already become familiar; it is all that is known. Although these children, when they grow into adulthood, may subject themselves to abuse in the form of career mediocrity or tolerate emotional or physical abuse by their spouses, for now they settle for other forms of self-torture. These may include eating disorders; for example, obsessive-compulsive rituals or even depression-induced suicidal gestures.

*Substance abuse.* For better or for worse, we often follow in the footsteps of our parents. If we grew up in a home where we saw people we admired cope with stress or disappointment by drinking alcohol or taking drugs, we learn that it is an acceptable alternative. When exposed repeatedly to instances where substances are used for relief or entertainment, we are likely to do the same when we have the chance.

Young persons raised in addictive environments have a greater likelihood of becoming addicts themselves and of choosing addicted persons as partners in life. Indeed, the legacy of addiction maintains a powerful momentum because of this phenomenon. In the previous chapters, we discussed students who are addicts and presented a four-stage model of how students become substance abusers. We want to emphasize here that abusing substances arises in part from a self-destructive urge to escape the pain, frustration, and shame of a difficult home environment.

*Eating disorders.* Eating disorders are described in three ways. Anorexia nervosa is characterized by significant weight loss and obsession with food, bulimia entails bingeing with forced vomiting, and pica is persistent eating of nonnutritious food substances (e.g., paper, chalk). The first two disorders are particularly prevalent among adolescent girls, whereas the latter is more likely among young children. Eating disorders are usually associated with extreme perfectionism, poor eating habits, and a distorted body image (e.g., an extremely thin person views his or her self as heavy). If left untreated, such seemingly innocent strategies as "overdieting" can prove to be permanently debilitating, even fatal. The victim will often pretend to eat to avoid causing undue alarm or may secretly vomit the meal once in private.

It is absolutely imperative that if you observe a child with unusually strange eating habits or an adolescent girl who has become exceptionally thin, you attempt to intervene. Although the first choice would be to speak to the child directly about your concerns, it may become necessary to make an involuntary referral because of the life-threatening nature of these progressive disorders.

*Suicide potential.* Children raised by parents who are addicted to substances or to anomalous behavior patterns (e.g., sexual obsession) are more inclined to have depression and to attempt suicide (Tharinger & Koranek, 1988). Once a person begins using alcohol and drugs, judgment is likely to be impaired. The future will seem more bleak. Impulsive behavior, especially of the destructive kind, is common. Once a child has had a few beers, or is otherwise in an altered state of consciousness, normal inhibitions are reduced. There is a much greater possibility that such a child will deliberately take an overdose, jump out a window, drive a car into a tree, or reach for a gun in the house. Many, many premature deaths that often seem like accidents are actually fairly well disguised suicidal acts.

You must stay alert to certain signs that a suicide attempt is imminent. Although the ability to predict such behavior, even by experts, is not very good, there are several specific indicators for students who have suicide potential:

- They show an increased use of drugs and/or alcohol.
- They lack a support system (few friends or voluntary withdrawal).
- They have a specific plan for carrying out the suicide (What? When? Where? and How?).
- They have the means to carry out their self-destructive plan (i.e., there is a gun in the home or sleeping pills in the medicine cabinet).
- They have begun attempts at closure (saying goodbye to people, giving away possessions, or clearing up loose ends).
- They have a history of self-destructive acts (previous threats, gestures, or attempts).
- There have been other family member(s) who attempted suicide (it runs in families).
- There are extreme mood swings, from depression to elation (signaling unstable conditions).
- They show significant changes in appearance and academic performance (they become sloppy, indifferent, or erratic).

Prevention of suicide is, quite obviously, most critical. Watching for these indicators and listening to these students, either directly (e.g., they tell you they want to die) or indirectly (e.g., rumors from other students), can alert you to possible suicide attempts. If you have created the kind of relationships with your students so that you are likely to hear about such despair, you may indeed save lives.

*Compulsive disorder.* Some children of addicts might demonstrate compulsive behavior at school. Such behavior results in repetitive behaviors (i.e., compulsions) for students that are seemingly uncontrollable. The rituals associated with these behaviors give them a sense of security and let them fend off difficult personal concerns and high levels of anxiety. As long as you are ruminating about the same idea over and over, or engaging in repetitive sequences of behavior, you are not thinking about other things that are even more distressing. Obsessions and compulsions give people an illusion of control over their minds or environment, even though, paradoxically, they are completely out of control.

The challenge you have in helping these students is recognition and intervention. For example, Trina is fastidious about her immediate personal environment. Before she begins work, everything has to be perfect (i.e., paper placed on the desk in a certain way, pencils perfectly sharpened and aligned, book arranged in the proper position). If this kind of behavior is indeed intrusive on your classroom environment, then you must do something. Because persons like Trina have extreme fidelity to their compulsive habits, they become anxious, nervous, and agitated when they are placed in positions of change. Special counseling may be needed for these persons (sometimes medication is helpful as well), especially when your requests to change the behavior cause excessive anxiety.

### The Fifth Challenge: Recognizing Escape Fantasies

The observable behavior of children (or any of us) is just the tip of the iceberg. We all live secret lives, private moments, that we have never shared with anyone else (Kottler, 1990). Furthermore, adults and children alike are mostly uncomfortable when they are alone. It is in solitude that we are most likely to engage in deviant acts, abuse ourselves, or abuse substances.

We need not be physically isolated in order to feel alone. Each of us has an inner world that we retreat into, a whole fantasy life that is both exciting and terrifying. In contrast with children who use their inner fantasies to spark creativity, goal setting, and healthy entertainment, those who are living within addictive environments develop fantasies that are inherently destructive to functioning. Berlin, Davis, and Orenstein (1988) report that these fantasies interfere with adolescents' normal separation from addicted parents and lead to anomalous relationships with persons outside the home. The fantasies become lifelong traps unless they are understood and addressed earlier in life.

*Nurturance fantasies.* Students whose parents are addicts rarely feel that they are cared for. Feeling rejected and unwanted is commonly reported by these students. To feel cared for and loved, they find a friend or caregiver who is sympathetic, and they tend to cling to this person in ways that are oppressive and socially unacceptable. In their inner worlds, they may pretend that these surrogate parents are real.

*Self-sufficiency fantasies.* Students raised by addicted parents or guardians can be fiercely independent and self-sufficient. Knowing that they survived the negative forces at home, they feel that they can survive anything. You can hear these young people say that they are "tough as nails." Self-sufficiency fantasy is particularly salient for young persons living in an environment where there are strong patterns of denial and the inability to self-disclose feelings.

*Perfectionist fantasies.* Some adolescent children of addicts have pressure put on them at home to represent the family in a praiseworthy way (e.g., make excellent grades, win awards at school). This takes attention away from problems at home. It also gives the semblance to outsiders that life at home is free from chaos. What ultimately develops, however, are overachieving students who are intolerable of even the mildest criticisms. Intimate relationships are also difficult for these persons; they don't want to let others break through their perfectionist facade.

*Revenge fantasies.* Young persons can be preoccupied with feelings of hate for their addicted parents. They feel hurt and rejected and may seek revenge for these feelings. Suicide, as described above, is one form of revenge for feeling betrayed. Adolescents can harbor this anger and hate and express it toward you through outlandish behavior in the classroom, toward peers through fighting and name-calling, and toward institutions like schools through vandalism.

This is but a sample of the fantasy life that children engage in while they are daydreaming in your classes. Look around your room at any given moment, no matter how interesting and compelling the lesson or activity, and you can be certain that more than half of the children are off in their own worlds, even as they meet your eyes and pretend to pay attention.

It is possible to help all children, not just the victims of addition, to use their fantasies for more productive rather than destructive purposes. This is true for getting the most from solitude in general, a subject that has been largely ignored in our educational system where we emphasize group coopera- tion but rarely teach children the appreciation and skills for occupying themselves when they are alone.

Teachers can help children get the most from their fantasies and time alone in a number of ways (Kottler & Zehm, 1993):

1. Counteract apprehensions and fears that come out when children are alone.
2. Encourage them to be more spontaneous and creative in their solitary play.
3. Discuss how they can entertain themselves construc- tively when they feel bored or restless.
4. Show them how to deal with feelings of loneliness and sadness in constructive ways.
5. Talk about alternative ways to relax when alone or when they need to recover from the demands of others.
6. Model ways in which you celebrate your own fantasy and inner life, demonstrating how you use your time alone most creatively and productively.

## Summary

In this chapter, we have described special classroom challenges to teaching children who now live, or who have lived, with addicted parents. These same challenges can also be applied to children who have become addicts.

It is both amazing and unfortunate that many children from these home environments do not even realize that their parents' addictions are particularly deviant, especially if it is all they have ever known. The inherent value of accepting the many challenges in working with these young persons in your classroom is to help them overcome their destructive urges, their patterns of denial, and to move them from a world of denigrating fantasies to wholesome reality.

Of course, we realize you cannot be a personal counselor for every one of these students. That in itself would be overwhelming both personally and emotionally, especially with all the other teaching duties you now have. But if you help even a few of these students begin changing their self-destructive habits, if you show them empathy, concern, and trust, you will have begun to reduce the powerful forces of addiction that pollute your classroom.

# 5

## Boundaries and Barriers: Understanding Toxic Families

One of the most exciting developments in working with victims of addiction is no longer treating them as if they are individual problems but rather examining their behavior within the context of their family systems. This means that the addicted person may often be the symptom of a larger family problem or the "designated patient." For example, the effect of a child's abuse of drugs may be that it pulls together otherwise conflicted parents who must cooperate in order to help their distressed family member. Another common scenario occurs when the addictive parent is inadvertently encouraged and enabled by other members who benefit from this scapegoating. In these and quite a number of other situations, it is impossible to understand what is going on with a particular child unless we have a grasp of the family dynamics.

### The Toxic Family

Chemically dependent families, those in which one or more members engage in active addictions, populate many homes throughout North America. It is estimated that in the United States alone, there are over 28 million children being raised in chemically dependent environments (Storti & Keller, 1988).

Such family systems are having profound effects on the emotional well-being and readiness for learning of thousands of young people in our elementary and secondary schools (Baird, 1991; Forward, 1989). The current rise in the number of youth runaways, crimes, suicides, street gangs, adolescent pregnancies, and drug use and trafficking all reflect the influence of addicted parents on the lives of young people (Metzger, 1988).

There are certain families that, as a function of how they are organized or how they operate, become poisonous settings for children to live in. These toxic families are known to have several characteristics that have been identified by family treatment specialists (Kaufman, 1985; Lewis et al., 1994; Madanes, 1983; Steinglass, Bennett, Wolin, & Reiss, 1987):

1. The rules that have been established are arbitrary and irrational. They are enforced inconsistently.

2. The boundaries between parents and children are permeable, creating confusion as to who is in charge.

3. The coalitions between family members are dysfunctional. One parent may be aligned with one sibling against the other parent who stands alone.

4. The power in the family is in the hands of those (usually the addicted members) who are not good decision makers.

5. Members relate to one another in ways that are neither direct or respectful. Communication is paradoxical in that mixed messages are often sent: Come close/Stay away or Stop it/Keep it up.

6. Triangulations exist in which the child is caught between the struggles of the parents.

7. Roles that members play are unusually rigid, not allowing for much improvisation or adaption.

8. Addictive behavior has become normative—the usual and customary way of dealing with problems.

9. The family is a closed system in that secrets are maintained and outside influences are not permitted to interfere with the dysfunctional patterns.

10. Family members are overly enmeshed or over-involved with one another. The identity of one member becomes infused into the other, making it difficult to separate who is causing what.

11. The symptoms of the addicted member(s) serve a protective function; they are the solution to a problem. As long as addiction prevails, members don't have to risk true intimacy nor do they have to assume responsibility for their lives.

12. The addictive symptoms are often a metaphor for other problems that remain disguised. Filling one's body with alcohol and drugs, for example, may be a symbolic gesture of administering love that is missing in more healthy ways.

13. The scenarios that are being acted out in this toxic family are often reenactments of struggles that have been played out in previous generations. Addictive behavior flows from one generation to the next.

14. Behavior in the toxic family is based on circular rather than linear causes (this is true of healthy families as well). This means that it is impossible to figure out who is at fault for the addiction; everyone plays a part in sparking dysfunctional behavior in the other.

As a teacher, you understand and appreciate better than almost anyone else the importance of a stable family to a student's school success. You know that the family provides your students with the nurturing, critical experiences and support they will need to live up to their potential as persons, students, and citizens. You recognize that when families function in healthy ways, they send you students who are ready for the challenges of learning. Contrast, for example, the student who walks in the door from school and is met by a caring family member who asks if there is any homework to be done with the student who enters the middle stage of a brawl.

Children who come from chemically dependent families are subtly initiated into a family cycle of addiction that will

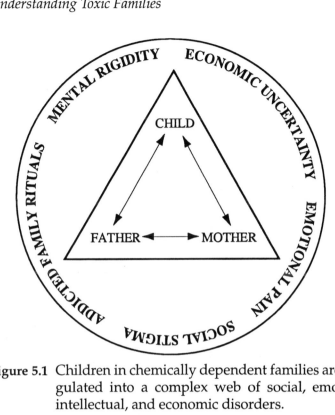

**Figure 5.1** Children in chemically dependent families are triangulated into a complex web of social, emotional, intellectual, and economic disorders.

interfere with their cognitive, emotional, social, and moral development. If left untreated, this arrested development will effectively rob children of their childhood, make the trials of normal adolescent development into an agonizing trauma of social isolation, and create havoc in all aspects of adult living and relationships.

Before you can intervene as a teacher to improve their dysfunctional classroom relationships, you must know how children and adolescents are triangulated into the problems of the addicted family (see Figure 1).

Once you understand how these circular dynamics affect all members of the chemically dependent family, you will be ready to understand how you are also subtly triangulated into this toxic system when a student from a chemically dependent family is enrolled in your classroom.

## A Toxic Family in Action

One of the first things you would notice about Amanda's family that might surprise you is that it is a highly structured family system. All families need structure to function as social entities. All families identify a variety of family roles assigned to each family member. These roles are established to assist families to function in purposeful ways. Amanda's family is no different from other families in this way; her family possesses a highly defined family structure as well.

If you were able to stay a little longer in Amanda's home, you would soon begin to recognize some key differences between the structure of toxic families like Amanda's and that of a healthy family. First of all, you would see major differences in the rules these families have set up to provide family structure. In a healthy family environment, the rules have been established to provide for the nurturance and well-being of all its members. The rules in Amanda's family have been established to take care of the addicted family member, their alcoholic father. The rules enable her father to remain under the influence of alcohol without anyone on the outside knowing the family's secret.

Wegscheider (1981) identified seven rules that subtly, yet forcefully, regulate the family systems of chemically dependent families like Amanda's:

1. The abuser's use of alcohol is the most important thing in the family's life.
2. Everyone denies that alcohol is the cause of the family's problem.
3. Someone or something else caused the alcoholic's problem; he or she is not responsible.
4. The status quo must be maintained at all costs.
5. Everyone in the family must be an "enabler."
6. No one may discuss the family secret either with one another or with outsiders.
7. No one may say what he or she is really feeling. (pp. 80-83)

In Amanda's toxic family, these same rules have been unwittingly set in motion to perpetuate the continued cycle. The father is allowed to continue his abusive behavior, whereas the mother is helped to survive the pain and spousal neglect that punctuates even those few apparently placid moments between the sobriety and drunkenness of her husband.

At this point, you are no doubt aware why Amanda will not bring to school the family security, happy relationships, or prospects for normal, healthy development that many of your other students enjoy. You may also wonder if the displeasing symptoms of disruptiveness, disrespect, laziness, and other classroom maladies displayed by other students have their roots in toxic families similar to Amanda's.

## Addicted Behavior at Home

The behaviors of children from substance-abusing families will give you clues to help you identify who these students are and how you can help them find success as students and human beings. Let's look at how the behaviors that Amanda and her younger brother Ricky have learned in their addicted family system influences their classrooms in quite different ways.

*Amanda.* At the age of 13, Amanda is 3 years older than her brother Ricky. As the eldest, Amanda has assumed many adult responsibilities. When her mother needs someone to help her accomplish what would ordinarily be expected of the father of the household, Amanda is there to offer herself. She mows the lawn. She takes out the garbage. When the neighbors observe Amanda doing these heavy lifting chores, they ask her why her father does not do them instead. "Oh, he's too busy doing other more important work." Amanda has learned to cover for him and would never dream of saying out loud what she is really thinking: "Because that no-good bastard is lying drunk on the floor, passed out after he tried to beat us."

Amanda appears to have a good relationship with her mother. She is her mother's primary source of support. When she needs someone to talk to about the anguish her husband is forcing on her, Amanda is there to listen. "I don't know what I would do without your help, Amanda," her mother praises her. "Without you, this place would be in total chaos." It saddens Amanda to witness the emotional abuse her mother receives at the hands of her father. "Don't you see all I have to put up with to keep this family together?" her mother, in regular fits of self-pity, shares with Amanda. "Don't you see why I need you to be my right hand?"

On the outside, Amanda appears to be the superresponsible right hand of her mother. She works hard to make her family appear normal. She works hard to earn her family's approval. On the inside, however, Amanda is filled with inadequacy and confusion. She blames herself for her mother's pain and her father's drinking. These feelings only make her try to work all the harder for approval that never comes.

*Ricky.* If you were able to observe Ricky in his home environment, you would not fail to notice a set of behaviors that appear to be totally unlike those displayed by his superresponsible sister. You would, no doubt, be struck by these radical differences in behavior. Their mother regularly shares her displeasure with both of her children. "Why can't you mind me like your sister does?" she laments. "She is so good and you are so rotten. You're going to grow up to be just like your father."

This kind of talk only serves to make this 10-year-old boy more defiant. On the outside, he is out of control. He runs around the house, screaming and tearing things apart. "I'm going to burn up all your toys if you don't stop throwing your things all over the house," his mother reacts. She often imposes harsh penalties to control the destructive behaviors of her son. Most of the time, her penalties are desperate threats on which she seldom follows through.

If you could tap Ricky's feelings, you would be overwhelmed by the repressed vortex of emotions that he keeps bottled up inside. First and foremost is anger. He is enraged by the rejection he feels from his alcoholic father. He is upset with his mother who rarely shows him any genuine affection. He resents the fact that she spends so much of her time rescuing her alcoholic husband and wallowing in self-pity, that she has little time left to care for the emotional needs of her children.

When Ricky is not acting defiantly, you will find him alone medicating his pain with schemes of running away. Many children of alcoholic parents his age actually begin soothing their pain with alcohol and other available substances they can steal from their parents. Ricky is on the verge of jumping, head-first, into his own life of addiction.

## Stereotypic Roles of Addicted Families

In the toxic family story of Amanda and Ricky, we shared with you the stereotypic roles that are prevalent. These popular role descriptions are currently used by therapists in assessing toxic family members and engaging them in treatment programs. In Amanda and Ricky's story, their alcoholic father played the manipulative role of the chemically dependent family member. Their mother assumed the role of the self-pitying chief enabler who rescued their father and maintained the family secret. Amanda fell into the role of the family hero who in the process of bearing the burden of becoming the superresponsible perfection seeker lost her childhood identity. Ricky played the role of the family scapegoat who acted out his pain and anger with defiance of parental authority and withdrawal into daydreams where he runs away from his family rejection.

Wegscheider (1981) has identified two additional roles commonly found in chemically dependent families: the "lost child" and the "family mascot." The lost child can be identified by behaviors that speak of isolation. The lost children in toxic families often pretend to be superindependent so that they can be alone and not forced to reveal their inadequacies. They often medicate their feelings of inadequacy and loneliness with food. Obesity is frequently a symptom of the effects on the lost child of toxic family life.

The family mascot seeks to protect him- or herself from the confusion and insecurity of his or her chemically dependent family system by doing anything he or she can think of to attract attention. Such children often appear to be hyperactive in their attempts to play the role of the family clown. They use humor to mask their pain and their own fragility. Underneath, however, the family mascot struggles with the same fear, pain, loneliness, and shame experienced by other members of his or her toxic family.

A final word is in order about these stereotypic roles assumed by members of chemically dependent families before we conclude this discussion. Remember that every chemically dependent family system is different. These role descriptions may be helpful in assisting us to understand how toxic family systems operate. They remain, however, stereotypes that may do damage to the individuals who are forced to wear these role labels and that may affect them for the rest of their lives (Baird, 1991).

### Behavior at School

*Amanda.* If you asked Amanda's teachers to evaluate her performance as a student in their seventh-grade classes, you would likely get a picture of a very successful student whose achievement is superior. "Amanda is one of my top students," her science teacher offers. "She is superdependable . . . she always gets her homework done ahead of time . . . she is always ready to do whatever is asked."

Her math teacher is, likewise, most enthusiastic about Amanda's academic performance. "Amanda is one student I can motivate to succeed without fail . . . she isn't satisfied with her work until she gets every one of her problems right! She sometimes bugs me by her drive to get the highest grades, but I'd rather have that kind of response than the noncaring, unmotivated responses I get from so many of my seventh-grade kids."

Amanda's teachers don't know her dreaded secret. They don't know that her classroom motivation is not prompted by love of learning or plans for the future. They are unaware that like her mother, Amanda is controlled by her father's addiction to alcohol. In her toxic family environment, she has become a codependent of her father's addiction. She brings the baggage of this influence with her into each one of her classrooms.

If you watch Amanda between classes and at lunch time, you will notice that she is an attractive and personable young lady, yet she spends most of her time alone. She avoids forming friendships for two reasons of which she may be unaware. First, she is afraid of revealing her family secret. This prevents her from initiating friendly contacts with her peers. Second, she is so dependent on the unhealthy relationship with the members of her toxic family that she is incapable of establishing healthy relationships with anyone else.

Observe her at work in the classroom. She attacks her individual learning tasks, driven not by an interior desire to perform well but by the compulsive need to be perfect and somehow make up for the shortcomings of her addicted father. In group activities, she will quickly assume a leadership role, do all the work, and let the remaining members of her cooperative learning group sit back and take it easy. She is used to taking care of people; this defines her existence. Again, her group behavior is not motivated by a genuine caring for her peers; it is influenced by the controlling behaviors she has learned in her toxic family environment.

Finally, scrutinize her interactions with her teachers, and you will recognize another pattern of behaviors that have been influenced by her toxic home environment. Amanda appears to be the ideal student to many of her teachers. She completes her work to earn the approval of her adult teachers. She is an astute manipulator, to whom most of her teachers would rarely give a grade of less than A, even when she might have deserved less. Perhaps they are afraid of disrupting the otherwise sterling performance of this academically talented student. Perhaps they know intuitively that any grade less than perfect would devastate the fragile self-esteem of this student. Her teachers have thus become triangulated into her dysfunctional family system.

*Ricky.* Amanda's brother is a fourth grader at the elementary school across the street from his sister's middle school. He brings into his classroom a pattern of behaviors that appears to be the exact opposite of his sister's approval seeking. Whereas she is the practiced teacher pleaser, Ricky gets attention in quite a different way.

"My life would improve 110% if Ricky were transferred from my class," his teacher painfully asserts. "I've tried every approach known to modern pedagogy and I am still unable to find any way to reach him," she legitimately complains. "We've done everything we can think of to help him. I've even referred him for special education evaluation, but they cannot find any evidence of specific learning disability."

When you ask his teacher to describe the behaviors that she finds so detrimental to Ricky's learning, she does not hesitate to list them. "First of all, he is the most sullen and disrespectful student I have ever had. I have students who will occasionally display belligerent outbursts, but Ricky is always obstructive . . . both to me and to all of the students in our class!"

If we were to observe Ricky at school, we would be able to verify the accuracy of this description. We would see him at recess stirring things up on the playground, fighting with other students. Not infrequently, we would find him in the principal's office being reprimanded for some obnoxious behavior.

These antisocial behaviors wear on the patience of his teacher and consume her precious instructional time. "I am getting so frustrated because no one can help me deal with Ricky's constantly disruptive behaviors. I've had two parent conferences with his mother (his father's work schedule wouldn't permit him to attend). His mother claims that Ricky never acts this way at home. She knows of no reason to explain his negative behaviors. In fact, she implies that I am the cause of his perpetual negative attitude. Give me a break!"

Ricky's mother continues to maintain the family secret in the parent conferences. His father's work schedule is hardly what interferes with his attendance; his addiction prevents him from participating. Ricky is exhibiting a behavior that professionals describe as counterdependence (Gabe, 1989). Because his personal needs for love, nurturance, and safety are not provided at home, he acts out rebelliously wherever he can. His only satisfaction comes from acting out his pain by inflicting his hurt on others.

### Recognizing Toxic Influence When You See It

Although Ricky lives in the same debilitating family environment as his sister Amanda, there appears to be a radical difference in style of adaptation. This difference demonstrates two important points that you must remember before you can be effective in reducing the negative effects of these children on your classroom.

First of all, remember that these children live in a very chaotic environment. The only consistency they know is the compelling certainty of the continuing addiction of a parent. The children raised in this unhealthy lifestyle will reflect in their unpredictable behaviors the same lack of consistent boundaries they find in their toxic families. That is one reason Amanda and Ricky are so different.

Second, remember that there are some common, typical, predictable indicators that children from toxic families will display. These students will often show a lack of trust that prevents them from forming healthy friendships with their peers. They can be very manipulative people, who learn to control others as they have been controlled in their toxic families of origin. On the one hand, they can be teacher pleasers, driven to perfectionism in their schoolwork. On the other hand, they can act out the abuse they have suffered by rebelling at home and at school. As loners, they find the space they need to maintain the family lies. They find a false comfort in not having to disclose their true feelings, even to themselves. If you remember these indicators, you might be able to recognize the Rickys and Amandas who populate your classrooms and open the door for them to a healthy student-teacher relationship.

### How Teachers Are Triangulated Into Dysfunctional Relationships

In beginning to recognize the harsh realities that face children and adolescents like Ricky and Amanda, you will also recognize that you, their teacher, are also sucked into their problems

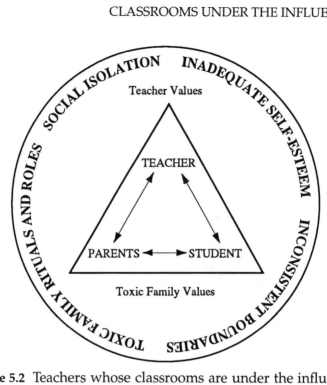

**Figure 5.2** Teachers whose classrooms are under the influence
of students from chemically dependent families are
triangulated into a complex web of social, emotional,
moral, and intellectual conflicts and disorders.

(see Figure 2). Your classroom is under the influence of children
from chemically dependent families. It is an influence that, if
left untreated, can rob your classroom of its safe and healthy
climate, can limit the effectiveness of all of your students'
learning, and can reduce the effectiveness of your instruction
and enthusiasm for teaching.

One of Ricky's former teachers was indeed triangulated
into the toxic family problems that Ricky brought into the classroom. What she learned, after much soul searching and professional assistance, will help others who are experiencing similar
violations of their personal and professional boundaries.

"I was Ricky's third-grade teacher. To this day, I don't know
how I survived that school year. But . . . looking back on it now,

I realize that in spite of all the pain, or maybe because of it, I learned an important lesson.

"My principal tried to prep me for Ricky's entry into my class, even before I had met him. 'Since you are one of my most caring teachers,' she prefaced her action with praise, 'I am confident that you will help Ricky find success in your classroom.' That is how I inherited this classroom terror without uttering one word of protest.

"It didn't take me long to recognize the symptoms of Ricky's previous school failures. He was always late for the beginning of class. He was frequently absent. He always complained about some physical ailment: sore throats or stomachaches. He had a temper of volcanic proportions, a temper that he regularly vented in sullen back talking toward me and in the punching and kicking of his classmates. With this kind of behavior, it is not surprising that Ricky was without friends at school. He spent his time alone.

"After enduring his disruptive behaviors for 1 week, I knew that I needed help. I called his mother for a parent conference. She came the next day. When I asked where Ricky's father was, I could tell from her lame excuses that a good part of Ricky's problems stemmed from something that was going on at home. I could tell his mother was filled with shame and embarrassment. She fooled me into thinking the source of this discomfort was the school behaviors of her 9-year-old son.

"I empathized with her ordeal of an 'out-of-control' son. I felt sorry for this beleaguered mother. After all, we seemed to share the same misery: We were both victims of this disobedient boy. When I asked her what she did to control Ricky's outbursts at home, she told me that only one form of punishment was effective: sending him to his room. We decided that I would try this same 'time-out' strategy at school until Ricky learned to behave himself.

"For the next 2 months, I used this strategy for dealing with Ricky's hostility and bullying. I created a special nook in one corner of my classroom for his time-outs. I even used a bookcase to build a wall between him and his classmates so that he wouldn't distract them. I wanted him to spend this time thinking about how he could improve his behavior so that he could rejoin the class.

"It didn't take me long to realize that Ricky did not want to rejoin the class. At first, this was okay with me; after all, I had 25 other third graders to teach who wanted my assistance. Later, when I began to realize that Ricky was spending more and more time each day in his corner, I began to feel guilty. I had effectively lowered my own professional standards by giving up on this 9-year-old. I began to feel some of that shame displayed by Ricky's mother for not being able to reach him. Although he wasn't disrupting the class while he was in his corner, he wasn't learning anything there either. I determined that I could either do better, or die trying. Little did I know. . . ."

Because this teacher was unaware of the reasons why Ricky was acting out, she was at a loss as to what she could do to be helpful. She did not know that Ricky's parents were using this report of his school failures to divert attention from the addiction of his father and the codependence of his mother. The teacher was also unaware that parents from addicted families frequently use the problems and failures their children experience at school to mask the problems and failures of the addicted parent(s) and the codependent family members.

It was not until many months later that the teacher finally learned that most of Ricky's disruptive classroom behaviors resulted from acting out his anger, fear, and feelings of abandonment toward his addicted family. Her first reaction at learning this cause was to reach out to Ricky's mother, who made her promise not to tell anyone about their family secret. When she willingly agreed to this, Ricky's mother promptly unburdened herself of years of shame and guilt, anger and despair.

Once she knew the source of Ricky's problems, the teacher did what many uninformed professionals are tempted to do: She got trapped into the same role expectations of Ricky's toxic family. She was secretive about the primary problem of his father's addiction to alcohol. She didn't even reveal to Ricky that she knew. She became overly helpful to Ricky and his mother. This teacher, now thoroughly enmeshed into the addictive parent-student-teacher triangle, had become a codependent of the family addiction. Her classroom was now eminently under the influence of an addicted family.

## Conferencing With Parents of Toxic Families

The chapters that follow will provide you with the tools you will need to intervene in your classroom to counter the negative influences of students from chemically dependent families. In these chapters, we will share with you strategies you can use to avoid becoming caught up in the disorders of addicted families that may compromise your effectiveness as a classroom teacher. We end this chapter with an examination of how teachers should conference with parents from addicted families to avoid the painful experiences that this teacher had.

As a classroom teacher, there is little you can do to directly intervene to bring an end to the addiction of one or more members of your student's family. Indirectly, however, there are ways in which you can use a parent conference to (a) recognize the possibility of a toxic family problem, (b) avoid becoming involved in an unhealthy working relationship with parents of toxic families, and (c) help toxic families identify resources they can enlist to end the cycle of addiction that will continue to damage each family member without appropriate intervention.

Based on the work of a number of family therapists, most especially the writings of Bowen (1982), Goldenberg and Goldenberg (1991), Haley (1976), Madanes (1990), Minuchin (1974), and Satir (1967), we offer the following guidance in planning your conferencing strategies:

1. Make sure both parents (and/or all stepparents) are in attendance, as well as the child.
2. Invite a school counselor, a psychologist, or a faculty member from the university to join you as a coleader of the conference if you feel hesitant about your skills.
3. Do not allow the child to be made a scapegoat and do not permit participants to place blame or fault.

4. Concentrate on the objective of allowing each person to present his or her side of what can be done to change things.

5. Make sure that each speaker is heard and understood before others are allowed to respond.

6. Try to reframe the negative behavior in a more positive light, focusing on the good that can come from addressing these issues openly.

7. Because you are dealing with a dysfunctional system, not a problem child, remember that changes must be made in the whole family.

8. Make note of family dynamics operating that might help explain the child's behavior.

9. Don't just concentrate on the content of what is being said but also on the underlying feelings that you sense are unexpressed.

10. Concentrate on helping the participants to have a good experience so that they will be more willing to consider ongoing family counseling when you make such a recommendation.

11. Focus on specific goals that can be reached within reasonable time parameters.

12. End the conference by allowing members to summarize what they accomplished and what they intend to do differently.

Keep in mind that treating substance abuse problems is among the most challenging of all cases handled by professionals in this field. It is not your job to repair these families nor to rescue the children. You are simply trying to learn more about what is going on in the family, enlist cooperation by the more sane members of the family system, and develop sufficient trust and rapport so that maybe they will take your advice and get some professional help.

# 6

## Taking the Right Path: What to Avoid in the Classroom

What is usual and customary for teachers to do with most of their students will not prove especially helpful with those who are suffering the effects of addiction. Many of these children will not do well with your normal class routines, nor will they respond to your attempts at control and discipline. Although you much prefer the children of addiction who take a perfectionist path rather than those who become rebellious, both groups will suffer in their own ways and neither will learn to be fully functioning adults.

What do teachers typically do when confronting problems of addiction? First of all, they ignore the problems, hoping they will go away. Because that almost never happens, they try a number of other strategies that are just as ineffective: scolding, blaming, arguing, punishing, the list goes on and on.

Before we suggest some classroom strategies to help you deal more effectively with children or adolescents who come from chemically dependent families, we think it is important for you to consider some caveats that may save you considerable time and anxiety.

### Don't Ignore

Ignoring the problem of your classroom being under the influence of addiction will definitely not make the problem go away. Do you remember the haunting musical strains of Ravel's "Bolero"? The music begins quietly, almost imperceptibly. But it soon begins to pick up intensity in volume and beat, losing its soothing rhythm to a distracting din of crescendos. That is what will likely happen to your classroom if you continue to ignore the problem. You will not only fail to reach those children who come from chemically dependent families, but you will also fail to reach children from healthy families who are being affected by the negative influences of their peers.

When you single-mindedly care only about your learning objectives, getting through your lesson plans, and covering the assigned material, you miss what is really going on in the hearts and minds of your students. If you recall your years in school, you know darn well that you were not all that interested in what your teachers thought was crucial. You had other more important things on your mind: what you would do after school, who you liked and who you did not, how you would perform on your sports team, where you would get the money you wanted, your grumbling stomach, the cute guy or girl in the next row, the teacher who didn't seem to like you.

Now imagine that you are the product of a toxic family. Your concerns as you sit in class are far more serious. Will your parents fight again tonight and keep you awake? Will your mom get high? Will your dad become violent? Should you go home or maybe find someone you can stay with? What is the stupid teacher saying now? Something about "sets," whatever they are. Maybe you could sneak some of the Jack Daniels your dad hides in the garage. Nah, they can smell it on your breath. Better to smoke a little weed. Your mom will never notice, she is so spaced out anyway. It would be nice to bring a friend home, but that is out of the question. For sure. What does that teacher want from you now? "No, I can't define what a set is. Does it matter? Just leave me alone. Fine. I'll go to see the principal."

Although we can't exactly ignore this child's behavior, as obstructive as it is, it is fairly easy to ignore what it means. After all, we have so many other children to look after, so many other things that have to get done.

You may not know what you can do about this problem, but you now know that ignoring things is not a reasonable alternative. This child's problems are only going to get worse, a *lot* worse, without some intervention. You are the person who is in a position to try and do something. The first step is making a commitment to no longer ignore the problems.

### Don't Blame

It is easy to find fault; there is enough blame to go around. It is the parents' fault for being so irresponsible. It is the child's fault for taking advantage of the situation. Can't the other relatives see what is going on? Why don't they do something?

Children from chemically dependent families are already overburdened with blame and shame inflicted on them by their toxic parents. Moreover, these children have burdened themselves with guilt; they blame themselves for their parents' drinking. Any additional shame you add to their lives may effectively destroy any chance you have of being a "significant other" in their lives.

Although we are not suggesting that you absolve them of all responsibility for their maladaptive behavior, your efforts will be more effective if you concentrate on figuring out what to do about the situation rather than blaming children for their misconduct or focusing on who is at fault.

Blaming creates a condition in which the other person is vested in defending him- or herself rather than looking honestly at what can be done to improve things. That is why, even if you don't get into a blaming mode, the child (or parents) may very well launch into a series of complaints on their own. If only we had more money, or more time, or more understanding, or more support from the school, or. . . .

Why don't we concentrate instead on what we can do if we put our heads together? Good idea.

### Don't Enable

It is interesting to consider the role that you play in reinforcing, inadvertently, the very behaviors you would like to eliminate. In normal speech, *enabling* is the term used to describe the role that a person plays to cover up for the chemically depend-ent person's inability to function socially or vocationally (Zelvin, 1993). This enabling behavior rescues the substance abuser, permits him or her to continue to cultivate his or her addiction, and enables him or her to escape the consequences of the substance-abusing cycle.

As the teacher of a student from an addictive family, you are also triangulated into the problems this student faces. Don't enable this student to continue to keep the family secret. Don't encourage your student to try to control his or her parents by hiding the liquor or exacting promises not to drink. These actions are subtle forms of enabling. Don't reinforce the belief that his or her parent's "little drinking problem" is controllable.

Within your own class, examine what you do to perpetuate approval seeking and perfectionist tendencies. How might you be encouraging obedience in favor of critical thinking, depen-dence instead of autonomy? Before you protest too quickly, really think about how safe it is in your classes for students to disagree with you. Consider how you may be perceived by them as conditional in the caring that you show.

Ask students what their teachers prefer, and they can spout off a long list of things that they can do to win approval:

"If you bring her food, she loves you. You get a free ride the rest of the day."

"Ask a lot of questions. That shows you are supposedly interested."

"Extra credit. Do all of it. Ask for more."

"Try to make them tell stories about their past. They love it when they can talk about when they were our age."

"Ask about their family. Remember the names of their kids."

"Bring in a book from the library that you are supposedly reading for pleasure."

"Tell them that you think they are a hard teacher. They want to hear that they are tough but fair."

"Stay after school to help them."

"Join the clubs they sponsor. Get other friends to join."

"Talk to them outside of the classroom. Call them 'mister' when you see them in the halls."

"They like to be right. Never prove them wrong. Even when they accuse you of something you didn't do, it is better to admit it to get on their soft side."

Interview *your* students about what they do to win your approval. What reputation do you have around the school as far as what you expect from students?

## Don't Victimize

If you have not been shocked already, you won't have long to wait to be devastated by the sad stories of neglect, physical abuse, and sexual exploitation suffered by children and adolescents living in chemically dependent families. What you must avoid doing, at all costs, is hanging an indelible label of "victim" on these children. This label and so many other deficit-oriented educational names ("slow learner," "at-risk student," "hyperactive child," "culturally deprived," etc.) often further victimize the child. They provide "scientific" excuses for the child and the teacher for students' lack of social, emotional, and intellectual growth. They permit us to set up a separate and lower standard of performance expectations for these students.

When we unwittingly continue to promote the victimization of children and adolescents from chemically dependent families, we effectively deprive these children of the hope of recovery for themselves and their families. We must always be supportive of the strengths, capacities, and resilience that these children and their addicted families possess (Jacobs & Wolin, 1991; Treadway, 1989).

Labels are often *dis*labeling. We call people names when we don't understand where they are coming from or we are frightened by the intensity of their emotions (Kottler, 1992). This occurs most often in the teachers' lounge when everyone gets together and complains, arguing who has the worst class or the most obnoxious student. Special education teachers favor acronyms to victimize—EMR (educably mentally retarded), SEH (severely emotionally handicapped), LD (learning disabled), VC (vertically challenged), PITA (pain in the ass), just as emergency room physicians speak cynically about their chronic patients, calling the elderly, intractable cases GOMERs (get out of my emergency room). In a more informal, but certainly no less colorful way, all teachers get together and talk about their problem students. The danger in this, besides creating labels that follow these children around for the rest of their school careers, is that we forever after respond to them as helpless victims who can do nothing to survive their plight.

## Don't Misunderstand

Don't misunderstand, misinterpret, or misdiagnose the classroom behaviors of children from chemically dependent families. Once you understand the messages of pain, anxiety, fear, rage, and neglect that they are sending, you will begin to realize how you can be an effective teacher and supporter of these students. When you truly understand what is going on, you will be able to help students like Ricky and Amanda deal with the guilt and shame their toxic families heap on them. You will help them to find ways to vent their unutterable rage and despair, give words to their anger, externalize their pain, and begin taking control over their own lives. Once you understand these children, you will be able to help them to redirect their anxious compulsions to be instantaneously perfect into genuine, balanced quests for excellence and self-acceptance.

Deep-level understanding of all your students, not just those who are suffering from toxic families or addictions, comes from a commitment on your part to listen to them, to really hear their stories. Although it may sometimes feel as if some children stay up late at night plotting ways to make your life miserable, they are often not responding to you. Just as therapists become the objects of their patients' transference (feelings that are projected onto people in positions of authority because of unresolved issues in the past), so too do teachers encounter this phenomenon in their classrooms. Many of your most hostile, uncooperative students don't even see you; they are acting out toward others in their life. You are a safer target.

Felicia, a middle school teacher, noticed that a student in her class seemed unusually angry toward her. In systematically reviewing the history of their relationship, she could think of no single incident that may have sparked this reaction. In fact, Felicia thought she had enjoyed a reasonably cordial relationship with this youngster.

Although her first inclination was to put her foot down and firmly put this student in his place, Felicia decided instead to try and reach some understanding of what was going on. During a brief conversation with the student, she learned that his parents had just decided to divorce; it was his mother's decision to move out. The student felt angry, betrayed, and hurt by his mother but did not feel it was safe to express these feelings to her, particularly because he believed that he was the cause of her moving out (a typical egocentric belief that is age appropriate). Felicia, on the other hand, was quite a visible target. Although this student was not even aware of what he was doing or why, he nevertheless began acting out his anger and hurt on this woman who resembled the mother he wished he had. Once Felicia understood these dynamics, she was able to respond to him in a more compassionate, controlled manner.

Another possibility that is considerably more likely is that most interpersonal conflicts, even those between students and teachers, result from a shared responsibility for the struggle. Interview the teacher, and he is likely to say something like: "I don't know what gets into this kid. I had him in sixth grade and he was a dream. He was my favorite student. Now, in eighth grade, he is gigantic pain. He has an attitude problem. He won't be quiet in my class. He is the source of a lot of trouble."

Ask the 13-year-old boy, and you will hear quite another version of the story, one that places blame firmly on the teacher: "She is crazy. That is simply not true! When she knew me in sixth grade, I had just moved here. I didn't have any friends. I was quiet because I didn't know anyone. Now I have lots of friends. Sure I like to talk. But I still do my work. I don't know what her problem is."

Part of understanding, therefore, involves examining our own role in creating conflicts within our classes. How do we inadvertently train or encourage some students to be difficult? Borrowed from another context (Kottler, 1992) in which therapists are urged to look at what they do to make their clients more difficult and uncooperative than they need to be, you might ask yourself the following questions when you are confronted by a student who is being uncooperative:

- What is it about this child that I am missing or not understanding?
- How is this child trying to communicate to me in a way that I am not listening?
- What issues of mine are interfering with my willingness or ability to be helpful to this child?
- Which personal issues of mine (i.e., need for control) are being triggered by this interaction?
- What rules have I set up in this class that are not working?
- What expectations do I have for this child that are not realistic or reasonable?
- Who does this child remind me of?
- In what ways have I been insensitive or inappropriate in the ways that I have acted toward this child?
- How am I exacerbating similar dynamics to a toxic family?
- What needs of mine are not being met?

Teachers often experience some defensiveness when they are requested to consider these questions. Each of them forces us to look at our own contributions to conflicts that emerge in classrooms, whether they are the direct result of addictions or any other problem.

### Don't Punish

When you feel inclined to use punishment as a potential remedy for the negative behaviors of the parents or family members of a chemically dependent family, stop and think about what you are doing. By punishing a child from a chemically dependent family for his or her acting-out behavior, you are only treating a symptom of the problem. In choosing to punish, you will undoubtedly add to the shame and pain this child is already suffering and further alienate him or her from a potential source of hope: an understanding teacher.

It was not only in our educational psychology classes that we learned that punishment is the least constructive of all interventions. (Remember: it causes either withdrawal or retribution, both of which are counterproductive to continued learning.) We have also learned, firsthand, that when we punish children we either shut them down, humiliate them, or escalate a minor skirmish into a major war.

The question is, then, If we should not punish, what should we do? We do not dispute that punishment is not an effective intervention in ceasing annoying or disruptive behavior. In fact, there is nothing that will work quicker than a good slap across the face, a cutting remark, or a bloodcurdling scream. The problem is in the side effects these interventions create. Although in the short run we have stopped the disruptive behavior, it is often at the expense of a student's dignity.

Perhaps some students have surrendered their dignity voluntarily by the very actions that they take. It is our job, then, to help them to restore a sense of responsibility for their behavior, not by lashing out but by doing one of a number of other things that we will discuss in later chapters.

### Don't Do What Does Not Work

There is a whole method of therapy that is based on the simple premise that when we are faced with problems, all we have to do is figure out what we are doing that is not working and not do those things anymore. Try something else, *anything* other than what you are already doing.

Usually a good place to start is to do the opposite from what you are already doing. Typically, if you raise your voice to a child, and you don't get the desired result, you yell a little louder; still no result, and you yell louder still. If you take away a child's privileges, and she does not respond, then you take away still more privileges, with similar negative results.

We therefore urge parents and teachers alike to make a list of all the things they have tried with an uncooperative child that have not worked. Such a list for a child who will not bring his books to class might look like this:

1. Remind him.
2. Scold him.
3. Write him a note.
4. Have him write himself a note.
5. Make him sit in the back.
6. Deduct points from his grade.
7. Call his parents.
8. Talk to his other teachers.
9. Send him to the principal.

As for our most challenging cases, none of these perfectly reasonable interventions proved to be successful. Does that mean that we know what *will* work? Absolutely not. But we do know what will not work. Because each of these strategies has already been tried numerous times, there is no longer any reason to use them again. It is clear they will not work. The problem, however, is that we get stuck doing the same ineffective things over and over again. We try something. It doesn't work. So we do it again. Harder. Longer. With the same result.

In all future efforts to stop disruptive behavior, the strategy is, then, to experiment creatively with other possibilities. Are we saying that any one of these will work? Assuredly not. Just add them to your list of things that do not work and keep trying until you discover the right combination of factors. In the example just mentioned, the teacher eventually discovered (about 3 weeks before the end of the year) how to finally get the child to bring his books to class. Because rewarding him for compliance did not work by itself, she first tried a paradoxical intervention in which she ordered him *not* to bring his books any more because he would probably lose them anyway. It was far better to keep them safe at home. She appreciated his caution in knowing his limitations. After he disobeyed her by bringing his books one day (probably by accident) she gave him special privileges that he quite enjoyed.

We are not saying that this particular strategy would work in another situation or that it would even work with him again the next year. The trick, however, to discovering innovative interventions is to let go of the ineffective things we are already doing.

## Don't Get Discouraged

Teachers are searching for solutions to the problems that children under the influence of addiction bring into their classrooms. When one solution does not work with an individual or group of students, they discard it and valiantly search for another. After failing to find a solution that makes much of a difference, many teachers become discouraged and give up.

Unfortunately, these teachers get trapped in the futile search for solutions to the problems of classrooms under the influence. In truth, there are no such solutions to be found. The issues are too complex. The problems are too pervasive. The challenge, therefore, is not to try to fix these problems single-handedly, but rather to do our part to reach as many children as we can.

# 7

## Breaking Through the Barriers: What to Do in the Classroom

**K**nowing what *not* to do is often easier to understand than knowing what to do. It is like having a map of a minefield that tells you which territory to avoid but offers very little in the way of guidance as to which ways you might go. This certainly helps you to avoid stepping on any explosive charges. Who knows, however, what other obstacles may be waiting?

One of the most insidious and predictable effects of addiction is that it not only fosters dependency in the addicts but also a sense of helplessness in those around them. When we see children who go home each day to a war zone, who are deteriorating before our eyes, we want to do everything we can to save them. Yet as hard as we might try, as patient, skilled, and loving as we might be, there are limits to what we can do.

### Making a Difference

At the end of the last chapter, we may have left you with some discouraging words when we said that teachers are powerless to solve the problems that students from addicted families bring into your classrooms. Addiction in our society presents a dilemma to every social institution that defies simple solutions.

Although it is true that you cannot solve the family problems that your students bring with them, you can help them learn to establish healthy relationships with you and their classmates. You can also help them acquire the coping skills they will need to begin to take better care of themselves.

From time to time, teachers talk about how wonderful it would be to have a homogeneous classroom of students who were all self-motivated, self-confident learners. You know that such musings are the stuff of fiction. You know that the real world of teaching means that you will always have mixed groups of students who have different backgrounds, priorities, and obstacles that they face. You also know that with all of the differences in student readiness, ability, experience, and attitude, the daily challenge that awaits you is, How am I ever going to deal with all of this diversity?

In the last chapter, we offered several caution signs to help you begin to deal with the challenge that students from addicted family systems bring into your classroom. Although you may find these warnings helpful to you in reflecting about the needs of students from addicted families, you will not always have the luxury of adequate time to stop what you are doing and reflect on these classroom "don'ts." If your classroom is an active laboratory of student learning, you no doubt operate under the green light most of the time. We urge you, however, to turn on the yellow light for both your students and yourself, slow down, and reflect about what you can do to make a real difference in the learning and lives of these students who silently cry out for your assistance. There is no doubt about this one fact: You can make a real difference in their lives!

## Teacher Efficacy

Most important among our list of recommendations about what you can do to make a difference in the lives of your students is your own sense of power as a helper. Unless you feel competent and confident in what you are doing, unless you know that you can make a difference, there is no way that you will convince anyone else, least of all the students you are trying to help.

It has long been established in the medical profession that the placebo effect is a powerful curative that often produces more miraculous recoveries than the most powerful chemical properties or surgical procedures. The same phenomenon operates, as well, in the practice of therapy (Kottler, 1991, 1993). When the helper, whether he or she is a physician, a counselor, or a teacher, truly believes in his or her power to heal and to influence and affect people in powerful ways, there is a much greater likelihood of successful intervention. In other words, *you must believe in your own effectiveness.*

Rather than focusing on what is not within your power to change—the child's parents or home life, the number and kinds of children in your classes, the limited resources at your disposal—we suggest that you concentrate instead on what you are able to do.

Members of the therapeutic community are often accused of spending too much time talking to people about what is wrong with their lives and not paying enough attention to what is going right. Therapists ask people: What is your problem? What is bothering you this week? Tell me about your troubles. What are you most concerned about? What crisis are you confronting? What's wrong? The emphasis is on looking at the most negative aspects of life, a request with which people are readily able to comply.

Teachers, as well, often spend a lot of time thinking about, and talking to one another about, what is not working and precious little time talking about the good things that are happening. Feeling effective in your efforts to intervene in the lives of children under the influence of addiction means believing in your own power to make a difference. It also means communicating to these children that they are powerful beings as well, perfectly capable of making the changes they would like. It means focusing on what is going right, as well as what is going wrong. Such a dialogue would sound something like this:

*Student:* "So that is why it all seems so hopeless. I don't see what the use is of even trying anymore. I mean. . . ."

*Teacher:* "One minute. I noticed that when we have these brief chats, it is mostly for you to tell me about all the miserable stuff that you have to deal with. I appreciate your trust and I like the fact that you can unload this stuff on me. We know the things that we can't do anything about, and it just makes us both crazy to talk about those things. You are stuck, for now, in your present home situation. We can't do much about that. Let's talk, however, about what you can do something about. Tell me, for example, about some of the things that have been going well for you. I saw you the other day with a new friend. . . ."

This direction toward the positive, to counterbalance the negative, does not ordinarily work very smoothly. People are vested in their habits of complaint. They are safe and familiar. They provide us with excuses to continue functioning below where we are capable. It is because resistance is likely that it is so critical that you believe in the power of what you are doing. Before a child can believe in him- or herself, it is first necessary that you believe in your own effectiveness as a teacher to make a difference.

## Training and Development

Once you realize that you do possess the power to make a difference in the lives of these distressed students, the next step is to seek the ongoing training that is required. Whether you organize such opportunities within your own school or attend substance-abuse workshops or graduate counseling classes, you will wish to learn how to relate to these students more effectively. This means learning a lot about family dynamics, patterns of addiction, counseling skills, treatment programs, prevention, and intervention.

We recommend that a school dedicate one entire school year to the mission of developing and implementing an action plan for providing for this segment of our at-risk school population.

## School Teams

The establishment of core teams of teachers can provide you with the training and support you need to be successful in working with substance-abusing students and codependent students from addicted families. These teams receive additional training to assist them in providing the leadership needed to work with other teachers, parents, and students in developing schoolwide student assistance programs.

A core team can help a school to spread the responsibility for help and develop ownership in a program to address the problems of chemical dependency in the classroom (Dean, 1989). Without this support group, individual teachers would soon burn out in the attempt to deal with classroom addiction problems alone. In addition to this structure, Dean recommends that schools also secure the services of a chemical dependence coordinator to work with the core team to accomplish the four following tasks: (a) provide information to teachers and students, (b) identify students who need help, (c) motivate families to seek help, and (d) provide support for recovering addicts and codependents.

Robert Ackerman, the cofounder of the National Association for Children of Alcoholics, has identified the following 11 areas of school concern that core teams can focus on to provide support to teachers and students from addicted families (Ackerman, 1987):

1. Helping students learn about alcohol and alcoholism
2. Helping teachers to deal with their own feelings toward alcohol use
3. Helping teachers to be perceived by their students as credible regarding alcohol use
4. Setting the right objectives for alcohol education
5. Developing a valid content for alcohol education
6. Involving students as active participants in alcohol education
7. Helping children of alcoholics express themselves

8. Helping children of alcoholics gain an appropriate identity
9. Helping students to relate effectively to alcoholics and nonalcoholics
10. Referring children of alcoholics to other services
11. Identifying children of alcoholic parents as part of an individualized educational program (pp. 82-83)

Although the focus of these content areas is centered around alcohol use and abuse, this agenda may easily be expanded to encompass all other problems of addiction.

## Classroom Management Strategies

Teachers in many schools are making a commitment to establish healthy relationships with their students to assist them in overcoming the dependent behaviors they have learned in their addicted family environments. They are making significant differences in the lives of students who appreciate the support they receive in their struggle to become centered, independent adults.

We wish to present to you the story of one teacher who has worked quite hard to create and nourish healthy relationships with his students, especially those who are reeling from the effects of addiction. He will speak to you in his own words:

"My name is Dennis Thompson, and I've been teaching language arts to seventh- and eighth-grade students for 12 years. In the beginning of my career, long before I ever heard the term "dysfunctional family," I discovered that a significant number of the students in my English classes came from disturbed family situations. Although no one ever identified these students for me, I came to recognize them in the patterns of behaviors they displayed in my class. Many were frequently absent. They often appeared to be depressed. They possessed low levels of self-esteem. They were very rigid students who could seldom be encouraged to take risks. Many had short fuses and would blow up in anger over the most insignificant stuff.

"Since neither my wife nor I came from dysfunctional families, I never fully appreciated the pain and shame suffered by students from these backgrounds. It took me a long time to realize that it was my ethical duty as a teacher to educate myself about effective ways of reaching these sad and discouraged students.

"The more I began to learn about chemical dependency and how it inevitably infects all of the family members, the more I understood about how I could manage my classroom to counteract these negative influences. I learned I could help these troubled students reduce the anxiety, pessimism, rigidity, fear, mistrust, and tension they bring into my classroom. When these negative influences were reduced, my classroom became a haven of learning for all my students, and for me as well!

"I realize now that my own upbringing in a relatively happy and healthy family environment prevented me from getting sucked into all of the problems that students from addicted families brought with them into my classroom. I learned that there were specialized strategies that I had to use consistently to successfully manage a class heavily impacted with many students from addicted families. I would like to share them with you.

*Consistent, fair rules.* "First of all, I learned the importance of establishing consistent, clear, and fair rules grounded on high academic expectations for all my students. With these boundaries in place, I encouraged all of my students to take responsibility for their academic and social behaviors. The consequences for failure to assume these responsibilities were also clearly delineated and I took pains to administer them with eminent fairness.

"I have to remind myself regularly that all adolescents I teach are in a state of glandular turmoil. I believe that the boundaries I established helped all my students understand the limits of acceptable behavior in my classroom. I am now convinced that it began to provide students from addicted families with the boundaries they needed, not only for success in school but for success in life. Although the boundaries I established for them in my class did not provide them with the rules and limits they needed at home to reduce the chaos of their addicted family system, they did give them a model for the present and future living of a life. They did provide them with a set of limits that supported their learning and personal safety at school.

*Climate of trust.* "The second strategy I use in managing my classroom to limit the potential negative effects of students from addicted families is to work hard to establish a climate of trust in my class. I learned from my study and observation of such students that they are not very trusting individuals. Raised in an environment of mistrust, they are taught not to reveal the fact that their mom and/or dad is an alcoholic or drug addict . . . they are taught not to trust anyone. Unfortunately, I have come to see that these students have learned to stuff their own feelings. They have also learned not to trust themselves.

"To counteract the distrust they bring into my classroom, I consistently attempt to model those behaviors that people in healthy relationships demonstrate. For example, I entrust my students with important elements of my personal life. When my daughter was born, I told them how I cried like a baby because I was so overcome with joy. I also shared with them the story of the shame I felt when the college professor of my Composition 101 class told me that if I improved, I'd be the worst speller in the class.

"Finally, I consistently enforce our class rule that states, 'No Plopping!' I believe that for all students, mutual esteem is the big brother of self-esteem. This is especially true in middle and junior high school where peer pressure is so intense. By not permitting students to dump their put-downs or petty jealousies on one another, I am able to build a climate of trust and manage my classroom much more effectively.

"Let me give you an example of how this works in my classroom. I use cooperative learning groups frequently to give students opportunities to brainstorm topics in language arts that we are reading or writing about. I select group leaders whose responsibility it is to see to it that (a) the group completes the assigned task on time, (b) everyone participates, and (c) no group member 'plops' on another by putting down their ideas. I found that when I learned to trust my students and when I managed my classroom with trust as an expectation of all students, they began to act in more trusting and supportive ways toward each other. This way of managing my class builds an alternative environment of mutual trust to counterbalance what they experience at home.

*Teaching about addiction.* "Within such an environment of trust, the third strategy I find useful is to focus the attention of my class directly and indirectly on topics related to addiction. As a language arts teacher, I can focus my reading, writing, and speech lessons on almost any topic. I find the topic of addiction to be a very interesting and productive one for all students. Everyone knows somebody who has a problem.

"When we first began to read and talk about the effects of addiction, I discovered that I could begin to help students from addicted families develop some of the important coping skills they needed to deal with the anger and shame they brought from home. I also found that students from addicted families could begin to find the words they needed to describe and vent their anger and shame. They did this privately within the pages of their confidential journals. Later, they even began to do it publicly in the safety of role-playing and creative drama activities.

"As a language arts teacher, I regularly evaluate the gains my students make in acquiring fluency in their oral and written language. I do not, however, evaluate the degree to which my lessons help students from addicted family systems cope. From time to time, however, I am presented with compelling evidence that reading, writing, and talking about addiction in my classroom is making differences in the lives of students. I've already told you that my students and I write every day in our personal journals. I do not read these journals. I intend them to be the private place where all of my adolescent charges can safely explore their own feelings. I'll never forget the day that Julie, one of my eighth graders, brought me her journal and said, 'Mr. Thompson, please read page 31 of my journal, and *only* page 31.' It was the beginning of her story about her alcoholic father. She trusted me enough to want me to know this about her. I like to think that Julie was beginning to learn how to cope with her family problems. Since that day, many of my students from similar family situations have confided in me about the pain and frustration of their addicted family life.

Having a relationship with an adult they trust helps them learn how to cope.

*Use of adolescent literature.* "The final strategy I use to reduce the negative effects students from addicted families bring into my classroom is to select and read adolescent literature to my students that focuses on the topic of healthy and unhealthy family living. One of the books that has been a part of our eighth-grade curriculum for years is Dickens's *Great Expectations*. This classic is still a powerful vehicle for revealing how young people like Pip, the main character, can overcome family obstacles and achieve their own 'great expectations.'

"Students also enjoy my daily reading sessions. I am pleased to find lately that there are many new books of fiction for adolescents that focus on the topic of family addiction. My students enjoyed Elisa Carbone's *My Dad's Definitely Not a Drunk*, a short novel about the revelation of a family's secret and the eventual recovery of an alcoholic father. They also liked Jay Bennett's novel *Coverup*, a mystery centering on possible criminal behaviors committed by young people who were under the influence of alcohol. I found Robert Cormier's thriller *We All Fall Down* especially effective in revealing to young people the progressive effects that alcohol has on the behaviors of people.

"Finally, I use selections from children's literature like Judith Viorst's *Terrible, Horrible, No-Good, Very Bad Day*, and Bernard Waber's *Ira Sleeps Over* as examples of how kids learn to solve problems in healthy families. I then ask each of my students to use these stories as models for writing their own children's books about how their characters can solve problems at home in healthy ways. After they have written their books and revised, proofread, and illustrated them, each student reads his or her book to a child in the elementary school across the street. I like to think that this participation in a literary activity may plant some seeds in the elementary child, and in my middle school student, that may help them both learn how to cope with dysfunctional family problems."

Although Mr. Thompson's narrative speaks of attempts to use classroom activities in middle school language arts classes, these same principles may be applied to any setting or age group. You are limited only by your own imagination.

## Being a Relationship Specialist

Dennis Thompson shared with you the strategies that he has found effective in managing his classroom impacted by the negative social and academic behaviors of students from addicted families. In addition to his four strategies, we would like to point out two other factors that make him very effective in working with students from addicted families: first, the daily effort he makes to establish genuine relationships based on trust with all of his students and second, the belief that all of his students will be successful.

In another book we wrote recently for teachers (Zehm & Kottler, 1993), we focused in one chapter on the important topic of being a relationship specialist. Within this context, our coauthor, Jeffrey, succinctly described what makes the classroom management strategies of teachers like Dennis Thompson so effective with all students:

> It is in our relationships with children that we earn their trust. Once they have decided that we are adults worthy of respect, they will follow us wherever we may wish to lead them—from the Peloponnesian Wars, Pythagorean theorem, and past participle to Picasso, Plato, and Pizzarro. Most children could care less about what we teach as long as they feel connected to us in some intimate way. (Zehm & Kottler, 1993, p. 43)

In addition to the effectiveness of Thompson's caring student relationships, the focus of his instructional efforts to promote the verbal fluency of all of his students has a very therapeutic effect on those from addicted families. Of course, he is not a trained therapist, nor is he trying to play the role of an armchair psychologist providing therapy to these emotionally disturbed students. In the context of his instruction in language arts, he is, nonetheless, helping students from addicted family systems develop the critical thinking and language skills they will need to cope with their stressful family situation and begin their own recovery.

Although he is unaware of it, Mr. Thompson's instructional approach is consistent with accepted treatment practice aimed at helping adult children of alcoholics (ACoA) recover from the effects of living in an addicted family system (Kritsberg, 1986). ACoA supports hundreds of groups across the nation in which the recovery of its members is supported by a program of three therapeutic components.

The first component is emotional discharge in which members learn to find the words they need to probe for and express their repressed emotions. This is what Mr. Thompson so effectively does in encouraging students to express personal thoughts and feelings in their daily confidential journals.

The second component of the ACoA recovery program is called cognitive reconstruction. It attempts to teach members who grew up in alcoholic families how to think in healthy ways that will enable them to live their lives free of the dependence that arrested the development of a healthy self-esteem. When Mr. Thompson provided his students with a healthy classroom environment, he gave students from dysfunctional families a model of a social environment based on mutual esteem where put-downs (No Plopping!) were not allowed.

The final component of the ACoA recovery process is behavioral action. Adult children of alcoholics are frequently mired in the same kind of chaotic lifestyles they lived in as children. Many unknowingly select spouses who were raised in similar environments. ACoA maintains that without a consistent program of behavioral action aimed at developing a healthy lifestyle, adult children of alcoholics will never end the cycle of addicted behaviors that disrupted their own childhood and added extra pain to their adolescence.

The classroom management approach of Dennis Thompson, grounded in quality instructional practices and caring relationships, was aimed at changing the social and academic behaviors of students. His focus on literary types of healthy families and their problem-solving practices gave his students from addicted families models of behavioral action they could use now and later in their adult lives.

### Action Plan for Managing a Healthy Classroom

Success stories can be helpful, but they can't be plugged in to our neural pathways to automatically reprogram us to become effective in our classroom management. It is up to us to finally understand that our classrooms really are under the influence of children or adolescents from addicted families and to develop an action plan to do something about it.

At this point, you have, it is hoped, begun to arm yourself with the knowledge that you need to understand the problems of children from addicted families and the challenges for teachers whose classrooms are under their influence. Knowledge alone, however, is not enough to help you build the repertoire of professional practices you will need to be consistently successful with these students.

In addition to knowing the dynamics of addicted family life, the stresses on children of addicted families, and strategies for effective classroom management, you will also need one more kind of support to help you adapt your instruction to meet the needs of this large segment of our school population. You will need a support group who can provide you with ongoing feedback regarding your effectiveness in developing caring relationships with these students.

The kind of action plan you choose to establish will also depend on your own needs. If you are a child of a substance abuser like the authors of this book, you will also need to direct much of the action of your plan to resolving those issues of your own addicted family background that may still be causing you major conflicts in your personal and professional life. If this is the case, there is all the more reason for you to seek the assistance of a trusted colleague who can mentor you on your classroom performance and who can also tell you his or her story of personal recovery.

## Summary of Things to Do

We offer a list of principles to remind you of the vast number of things you can do to make a difference:

1. *Be observant.* Watch your students carefully, not just for evidence of academic deficiencies or behavior problems but also for the subtle signs of addiction and emotional distress. Remember that it may very well be the most quiet or cooperative students who are struggling the most.

2. *Be flexible.* Classroom rules that are too rigid and unyielding may invite students to act out. Those who already feel so oppressed at home are chomping at the bit to find ways that they can flex their sense of power. Flexibility ensures that you can adapt as situations change.

3. *Set boundaries that are enforced consistently.* The other side of the coin is that although some students will resist limits, there will be others who desperately need predictable structures. When chaos exists at home, some sense of order is crucial at school.

4. *Deal with process and content.* Monitor the psychological, as well as the academic, climate of your class. Find ways to help children look at the way they do things, in addition to the acts themselves. Invite children to explore the ways in which they relate to others and to you.

5. *Make addiction a focus of discussion.* Bring this important topic up as often as you can. Regardless of your content area, find a way to deal with this subject as part of what you do.

6. *Make it clear you are available.* Communicate through direct invitation, and by your behavior, that you are eager and open to talk to children who want some help. Give your undivided attention. Let the child know how honored you are by their trust.

7. *Develop a referral network.* Because you are not trained or prepared to administer treatment, your job is to develop enough influence so that you can make a referral to the

appropriate professional and have the student follow through. This means you will need to develop contacts with counselors, psychologists, and social workers in your system. It also helps to know about outpatient and inpatient treatment facilities.

8. *Try family conferences.* Rather than doing just parent conferences, invite everyone in the family to come for a conference. Find someone with some expertise (a school counselor or a professor from the local university) and work to help family members work together as a team.

9. *Initiate an intervention.* In the parlance of substance abuse treatment, an "intervention" is a dramatic, decisive attempt to confront the abuser by gathering together everyone in the person's life who has been affected by the addiction. This includes immediate family, extended relatives, friends, neighbors, school personnel, social service or probation personnel, and mental health experts, anyone who can play a role. Your job is just to get the ball rolling, not to lead the meeting.

10. *Reach out to the troubled child.* Don't wait for him or her to come to you. Once you observe that someone may be struggling, approach the child in such a way that you are not intrusive. In a gentle and caring way, you are simply communicating, "I notice that you seem to be having some difficulty. I just want you to know that I care about you. I want to help. I want you to call me any time you are ready to talk. And if you would rather speak to someone else, let me find you someone you can trust."

11. *Detoxify yourself.* As we have said repeatedly, classrooms under the influence of addiction are poisonous. You, too, have been affected adversely. That is the source of your cynicism, fatigue, helplessness, frustration, and signs of burnout. Take care of yourself. Do what you need to do to feel good about yourself and your work.

12. *Accept what you can do little about.* You can't make people stop drinking, taking drugs, or anything else. They have to hit bottom, to become so desperate they are willing to do

anything to get better. Your job is to help that to happen sooner by not enabling their dysfunctional behavior.

13. *Work to change the family system of your school.* As you well know, a professional staff can be as dysfunctional as any toxic family. Coalitions, power struggles, bickering, verbal abuse, inept supervision, poor morale, and out-of-whack priorities are unfortunately all too common. Do what you can to initiate changes in your "school family" so that your organization becomes a more fully functioning model for children.

14. *Confront dysfunctional colleagues.* This is a risky action that most people do not have the courage for. That is why we knowingly permit colleagues, who we know are out of control, to continue to do damage while we look the other way. It is not only ethically professional but socially appropriate to bring to a colleague's attention behavior that is both self-defeating and destructive to students. We all know colleagues who have problems with drugs, alcohol, gambling, and other addictions. We owe them, and their students, to try to do something about their predicaments.

Finally, we urge you to create a vision of the ways you would like your classroom and school to be. We presume this is an environment that is free of addictions and their poisonous effects. Although attempting to rectify these problems in a remedial way is certainly important, by far the most successful efforts are aimed at prevention.

# 8

## Everyone Can Win:
## Toward an Addiction-Free
## Learning Environment

What responsibility do you have as a teacher to intervene and prevent the dysfunctional behavior of students whose parents are addicts or of students who are addicts themselves? We have heard some teachers argue that their job is not to be a classroom counselor; they say that they have enough work to do without contending with these problems as well. Other teachers, however, feel it is their job to do all they can for students at both personal and academic levels.

A premise underlying this book is that whether you choose to address these issues or not, a number of your students are dealing with problems of addiction every day. Although students' problems might not be openly talked about in the classroom, and although students might not come to you personally with their dilemmas and traumas, you nevertheless deal with their mood swings, their low self-esteem, and their attempts to cope with the social rigors of school in the shadow of their home environments.

When you teach students, you deal with the behavior they have learned from coping with their home environment. That is why some students are wonderful to work with; their homes have provided them with comfort, safety, security, and a positive self-image. And that is why other students, such as those from homes where chronic addiction prevails, pose different challenges for you. Their homes have provided them with discomfort, fear, insecurity, a negative self-image, and low self-esteem.

Students at school are unable to put aside the habits, customs, and coping behaviors they learned at home. This chapter is intended to help you recognize these coping behaviors and, whenever possible, do things a bit differently in your classroom for these students. First, in a discussion of enabling behaviors, we consider how you could actually be aggravating problems for students who are being influenced by the addiction phenomenon. We then suggest how you might work to prevent inappropriate behavior from these students. In the third part of this chapter, we suggest an assessment and intervention model you can use in your classroom for helping children of addicts. Finally, we offer suggestions for helping you better understand how your own addictions, if any, affect your classroom learning environment.

## Enabling Behaviors

### Making Problems Worse

We mentioned earlier that teachers sometimes inadvertently encourage students to maintain and perpetuate inappropriate dysfunctional behaviors in the classroom. This dynamic of "enabling" is similar to what happens in the child's family itself—we may think that we are being helpful, but we are actually making problems considerably worse. This occurs, most often, when we allow students to get by with a lack of effort or with irresponsible behavior (Landfried, 1990).

The ability to stop enabling behavior is predicated on the principle that you know when students are acting dysfunctionally. Although the obvious examples of this are behavior and discipline problems, which you could hardly miss, we have also mentioned the overadaptive versions whereby students become perfectionist, approval seeking, and excessively achievement oriented. Indeed, there are very few teachers who would say to themselves in response to an overly obedient, placating, perfectionist student, "Gee, this kid has problems. She is *too* good. I'd better help her to slow down."

We have included below several key points to remember about classroom enabling. Remember that when children who live with addiction come into your classroom, they think that they are basically unworthy persons, that no one would love them as they are, and that their needs are probably never going to be met if they depend on other persons. These students come to your classroom, then, with low self-esteem, a poor self-image, and extreme self-reliance. Consequently, they have acquired survival behaviors that may or may not fit well into your classroom environment. The points below are intended to help you develop insight into the enabling process. They are also intended to encourage you to reflect on your own classroom behaviors relative to this issue.

### Remaining Uninformed

Remaining uninformed about addiction, and its implications for school, contributes to the presence of enabling behavior. Teachers who are personally unfamiliar with the addiction phenomenon (i.e., who haven't experienced it firsthand) and who have read little in this area may be naive about its processes and products. The first step to learning about addiction is to read more and to talk with others who have more experience. This book is just the beginning.

### Ignoring the Problem or Behavior

A second type of enabling behavior occurs when you ignore problems students have, hoping they will go away if you overlook them long enough. As an example, Khadisha rarely participates willingly or actively in your class activities. You know from other teachers that her father is a chronic alcoholic. There are also rumors that she has been sexually abused at home.

Although Khadisha has completed some excellent assignments for you, her work is usually below average. She is not a team player in group work but rather is very quiet and withdrawn during these times. You become aware that since the second month of school you have not noticed her much, knowing she won't participate even if you ask her nicely.

Students like Khadisha are perplexing. You know they have the potential to do well, but they are so utterly withdrawn that even your best resources are unable to draw them into your lessons. Deutsch (1982) gave the name "lost child" to unobtrusive students like this. In their homes, these children have learned that by appearing inadequate and quiet they cause no problems with parents who are already overmatched. They see it as their primary mission in life not to draw any attention to themselves. After all, for them attention is associated with being abused. When you overlook and ignore them in your classroom, you enable their dysfunctional behavior they learned at home.

### Assessing Your Interactions With Students

A third type of enabling behavior for classroom teachers is to treat the whole class as one student, rather than viewing each child as an individual. Students like Khadisha represent one way that children adapt to toxic family situations. To pinpoint other children who might be struggling with their own issues, it is necessary to "take the pulse" of each one. Make a list of students like Khadisha, whose names you often tend to forget. Then make a list of students who constantly cause you the most problems—the class clowns, the disruptive influences, the belligerent, noncompliant ones, the students who don't stop talking, who don't follow directions, who constantly need to be the center of attention. Finally, note those students who always seem to be hanging around your desk, who bother you constantly about their grades and making perfect scores (true, *every* student in your class may end up on your master list).

Although not all of these students are under the influence of addiction, because there may be a variety of other factors that perpetuate this behavior, the possiblity of drug and alcohol problems in the home is certainly a reasonable hypothesis. We also want to be careful with "false positives," or overdiagnosing this problem. If the filter we look through is one in which we are constantly searching for problems of addiction, we may very well see it where it does not exist. Children may, in fact, learn that if they want special sympathy or breaks from you, all they have to do is complain about their crazy home life.

Nevertheless, each of the behaviors described above *may* point to the possibility of a dysfunctional home environment. From your inventory, do you notice that some of these students require more of your attention in and/or out of the classroom than others? How do they attempt to gain your attention? In what ways, if any, does your interaction with these students actually promote their inappropriate behavior? Using these questions to reflect carefully about your interaction with individual students is the first step toward overcoming enabling behaviors in your teaching.

### Classroom Prevention

The key to preventing classroom problems related to addiction is to look at the big picture. If you attempt to intervene in the life of every child, you will run yourself ragged. Scales (1990) has mentioned the value of concentrating instead on the broad development of cognitive, behavioral, and social capabilities. This moves away from the didactic approach of telling students what they should and should not be doing with their lives and moves toward a holistic, compassionate, and collaborative approach to helping students (Walter et al., 1991). This also allows you to address classroom problems from the standpoint of the whole child and not only the isolated behaviors they exhibit.

You might be saying, "But I *already* focus on the cognitive, behavioral, and social capabilities of my students." Indeed, good teachers do these things naturally. What we want to emphasize, however, is that by knowing who the at-risk children are, you will be better prepared to recognize that normal behavioral, social, and emotional development are interrupted.

### Modifying Existing Strategies

Let us emphasize once again that we are not suggesting that you make wholesale changes in how you deal with students in your classroom. Given the daily demands of your teaching, this would be an unreasonable request. We do suggest the following:

- Begin reflecting carefully on how you interact with young people in general, and with those who seem to be perplexing, enigmatic, or bothersome in particular.
- Consider whether or not these students are living in an addictive environment.
- Take an inventory of your interactions with these students and of your views of addiction, substance use, and substance abuse.

Students who pose extreme behavioral and emotional problems in your classroom should obviously be referred to school counselors or other professional staff for special prevention and counseling programs. Others who are struggling in some way (e.g., withdrawn, class clown, compulsive overachiever) but who don't warrant referral to special counseling may change their behavior if you modify your existing classroom strategies. We would like you to reflect carefully on the strategies you are currently using to see if they are appropriate for the students we are talking about in this book and to check that the strategies are not enabling students to maintain dysfunctional behavior in your classroom. Kottler and Kottler (1993) suggested that refining some of the skills you already have can help you maximize your responsiveness to students.

*Attending.* In the fast pace of the classroom, it is often hard to give individual students your full attention, if only momentarily, when you have so many things to monitor and manage. As former teachers, we admit that we often spoke to students in passing or talked to them as we graded papers or did other tasks. Attending means giving students your whole attention with your body, face, and eyes. Because students of addicted parents are accustomed to being devalued at home, attending to them in your classroom gives them the message that you care about them and that they are worthy of your full attention.

*Empathic resonance.* One goal of this book is to help you develop empathy for, and understanding of, children affected by the addiction phenomenon. This means communicating with students in such a way that they feel not only heard but understood by you, so that they won't feel so isolated and alone.

*Questioning and self-disclosure.* Questioning students empathically, reflecting content and feelings to them, and disclosing your own feelings whenever appropriate helps you to explore what students are feeling in your classroom and lets them know what you feel. The value of these actions is in the potential they have for establishing an open, trusting atmosphere for students in general, and for your personal interactions with students of addicts in particular.

*Giving advice to students.* One reaction you might have if you discover that one of your students has an addicted parent is to hurriedly give the student advice. As adults, we feel that we have a right to give young persons guidance about their life. And in certain instances, we should give advice, such as when a student is engaging in behaviors that are obviously self-destructive. For children who live with addicts, however, giving advice can do harm to their lives. In many instances, students of addicted parents already have some idea of what they should be doing, and most certainly what they would like to do for and with their parents. What they need is someone who is willing to listen, attend, and be empathic. As a classroom teacher, you are in a position to do this.

Giving students advice about what they should be doing about their home life can be risky unless you are familiar with various forms of addiction and with the unpredictability of addicts. If you have an inclination to give advice to students, or you have already been doing this, we suggest that you might consider operating differently. Rather than giving advice, help students set goals for themselves, help them understand how their inappropriate behavior can be changed, and help them develop a plan to alter their inappropriate behavior.

*Encouragement.* What if Khadisha, the withdrawn child mentioned previously, eventually makes progress in participating more in class? What if your class clown, whose mother is an alcoholic, begins controlling his comic outbursts in class? Not only do these students need honest, loving encouragement to change their behaviors, they also need support to continue these changes. By affirming these students as worthwhile persons in their effort to make changes in their lives, you can help them begin moving away from their dysfunctional behaviors in small but significant ways.

## Assessment and Intervention

Helping students from addicted environments in your classroom, and eliminating any enabling behaviors you might be demonstrating, depends on an assessment of student needs and a classroom intervention plan that has been carefully developed. Below is a model you can use in your classroom to assess the needs of students in addictive environments. Although the model was first described in relation to adolescent children of alcoholics (Powell et al., 1994), we have expanded it to work with all students who might be living with addicted parents, as well as those children who are addicts themselves. The steps in the model include (a) gathering information, (b) analyzing information, (c) planning an intervention, (d) implementing the intervention plan, and (e) following up the intervention.

### Gathering Information

Three types of information are needed for assessing the needs of students in addictive environments: student information, teacher information, and classroom information. To gather student information, use your intuitive sense about students to develop hunches. You know when something is not quite right with a student; you can *feel* it in your gut. When you develop such a hunch, seek out other information, such as student records, counselor reports, and observations from other teachers or students. Monitor student behavior over time and, when appropriate, make a phone call to talk with a parent, the one who, it is hoped, is least affected by the addictive effects.

As you gather information about students, reflect on your interactions with students as well, to identify possible enabling behaviors. Take a close look at the social, cultural, and academic climate of your classroom. This gives you information about how a targeted student might be influenced by your whole classroom dynamics. Also reflect on how your classroom environment is being influenced by students.

While you gather information about students, yourself, and your classroom, think about the whole phenomenon of addiction. Gather additional information from local, state, and national organizations about drug and alcohol abuse. Explore various forms of addiction, such as sexual addiction or workaholism. Consider how these lifestyle addictions also affect your students in ways similar to substance abuse.

### Analyzing Information

After you have collected information from various sources, you then need to reflect carefully on what you have learned. Determine if all sources of data point to the need for changing the way you work with a particular student. That is, do reports from other teachers about a child's classroom behavior, your particular interactions with the child, and your growing awareness of the addiction phenomenon suggest collectively that the child is from an addictive environment? If there is no such indication, and you still have a hunch the child needs special attention, you might consult with the school counselor for further guidance. If there is some indication, then additional student information might be needed over time.

### Planning Intervention Strategies

You want the most optimal classroom learning environment you can possibly establish. Once you have targeted a student from an addictive environment, you will be eager to plan and implement some action plan, both for yourself and your student. This strategy will need to be something that you can reasonably and realistically implement within your time and resource parameters.

You will wish to consider several decisions in your efforts:

1. *Decide the goal for the intervention.* What is the goal for the intervention plan? How will you know when the goal has been reached?
2. *Decide parameters of the intervention.* Where will the intervention begin? Who will begin the intervention? How long will it last?
3. *Decide how information is presented to the student.* Who will approach the student with the intervention plan? How will the student be approached? How will confidentiality be assured for the student? What information will be presented to the student so that he or she won't be afraid or mistrustful?
4. *Decide whether parents will be involved.* Will parents be involved in the intervention plan? If yes, then how will they be told? Who will tell them? What are the implications of telling parents?
5. *Decide the strategies you will use.* How will the student be cared for? In what ways will you, as a teacher, change your behaviors toward the student, and how will the student know about these changes? What will be the consequences for the student if he or she fails to comply with the plan?
6. *Decide strategies for building self-esteem.* Given individual students' needs and classroom behaviors, what activities are best suited to helping targeted students feel safe within the intervention plan so they can change behavior safely while building self-esteem in appropriate ways?
7. *Decide changes in classroom climate.* What enabling behaviors will you change? What changes must you make in the classroom climate to accommodate the intervention plan?

## Implementing the Intervention Plan

Only after the plan has been carefully thought out and after the questions above have been addressed thoughtfully and with sensitivity should the plan be attempted. Successful implementation depends on several key factors:

- Maintain an atmosphere of caring and concern.
- Establish clear ground rules for the intervention. Let students, and others who are involved, know the rules.
- Let students know the goals for the outcomes. Involve them in developing the goals.
- During the intervention, tell students how they are doing. Give them facts, not just opinions. Students can't argue with facts.
- Help students stay focused on the intervention plan. Avoid making unnecessary changes in the plan.
- Be clear about consequences for not achieving goals of the plan.
- Don't threaten students with the intervention plan. The plan is intended to help, not induce fear or anger.
- Don't bargain with students about the plan after it has been implemented.
- Don't make judgmental statements about students' home lives or their classroom behavior.

### Following Up the Intervention

To be successful, the intervention plan should include some kind of effort to evaluate the results. Let students know about how you will be following up the plan. Let them take responsibility in the follow-up. Ask what would be best for them. Build checkpoints into the intervention strategy over time so that progress can be assessed. Give students clear time lines for achieving the goals of the plan, and let them know how and when you'll be following up.

### Confronting Your Own Addictions and Codependency

So far in this chapter, we have focused on strategies you can employ for helping students in your classroom who are living with and around addiction. In this last section, we want to focus on *you*, the teacher, and explore how your addictions, if any, might be affecting your classroom learning environment. We also want you to consider how your prior and/or present life with an addict might be influencing your attitudes and behavior.

Our intent is not to create more shame regarding your own behavior. We are interested, however, in turning up the heat to increase discomfort levels with addictive behaviors that may compromise your ability to be as effective as you can, both as a professional and as a human being. In order to have an addiction-free classroom, the first place you must start is with yourself. What habitual behaviors do you engage in that are not good for you? This not only includes obvious addictions to drugs and alcohol but also tendencies to abuse your body with tobacco, unhealthy foods, or lack of exercise. It could also include aspects of your lifestyle that are not necessarily self-enhancing.

Earlier, we mentioned how licit substances affect your daily mood swings, just as these substances do for students. Caffeinated drinks, sugared colas, candy bars, chocolate, and tobacco are addictive. They influence moods, get us going in the morning, and keep us artificially alert.

However, teaching is a high-stress job. Hundreds of decisions are made each day about students' classroom lives. Burnout is high in the teaching profession. Prescription tranquilizers soothe the stress and help teachers unwind at the end of the day. Yet even though they may momentarily remove the anxiety that comes with stressful lives, these tranquilizers are addictive.

There is nothing easy about giving up addictions. When an addiction influences your classroom instruction, your interactions with students, and your interactions with professional peers, then you must address it if you hope to be a legitimate model for your students. Below are six suggestions for confronting your own addictions, and for dealing with your co-dependency habits and behaviors.

## Be Honest With Yourself

Before doing anything about your addiction or codependent tendencies, you must be open and honest with yourself about them. It occurs to us, as we are writing these very words, that although we have been relatively successful in avoiding the same pitfalls that trapped our parents, we are all qualified workaholics. Each of us is making progress in this area, especially as we age and diversify our lives. Nevertheless, denial of this problem allowed us to continue an overstressed existence in which we medicated ourselves with work rather than drugs.

Unfortunately, many persons who live addictive lifestyles are unable to admit the extent of their problems. Some of you are even reading these words right now, saying to yourselves, "None of this applies to me." You might as well skip this section, right? Wait! We are talking to *you*!

Only you know what you do in the private moments of your life and whether you engage in self-destructive addictive behaviors during these times. Addiction usually means that part of your behavior has gone underground and that in solitary moments some of you compulsively and obsessively indulge in self-destructive habits.

Once you have owned your addiction, you will be in a position to do something about it. Does your addiction make you nervous and agitated at times throughout each day? Do you sneak away from the school during the day to indulge in your habit? Do you recruit others to participate in your addiction? Does the stress of living with an addicted spouse cause you to be unnecessarily angry with students?

Teachers, just like students, are fallible. But fallibility does not have to mean defeat and self-denigration. On the contrary, addiction and human imperfections provide us with pathways for growth and development. Honestly admitting addictions to yourself, and eventually to other persons you trust, will help you begin moving away from your self-defeating behavior.

### Address Unresolved Family Issues

Teachers who are living with an addict, who were raised by addicts and were abused by their parents, or who are struggling with an addiction may have unresolved family issues that need to be explored. Although you are very capable of reflecting on your past family issues, dealing with these alone may be less productive than enlisting the help of others who are skilled in these issues, especially if your unresolved concerns deal with serious abuse you experienced earlier in your life.

Most teachers enjoy medical benefits that pay for counseling and therapy. There is a good reason for this because we are in positions of such power and influence. If we are not functioning at our best, if we become emotionally impaired, it will definitely affect what we do in our classrooms.

Seek the services of a professional for a tune-up, even if you do not require a major overhaul. Each of us gets back into counseling every few years, not because we necessarily need it but because it feels good for someone to challenge us to reach higher levels of personal growth. If you do not know of a professional who is especially skilled at working with teachers, consult with your school counselor or a friend for a referral.

## Join a Support Group

Confronting and dealing with your addiction alone is an arduous task. Few of us have the willpower and stamina to overcome our addictions alone. Through denial and rationalization, many addicts return to their habit after trying many times by themselves to give up the habit. Support groups provide you with extra care when your inner strength for recovery runs out. Groups such as Alcoholics Anonymous, Adult Children of Alcoholics, Al-Anon, Narcotics Anonymous, Sex Addicts Anonymous, and Workaholics Anonymous are all composed of persons with similar interests who want to give up an addiction or break free from the stronghold of codependency.

Because there is tremendous variability in the quality of these groups, depending on their focus, composition, and location, you will want to experiment with visiting several before you find one that provides a good fit for you. There are groups that emphasize or de-emphasize spiritual aspects of recovery, and others that do not permit smoking. Depending on their location, some groups attract quite diverse populations. Take these factors into consideration so that you do not give up after your first few attempts to find support.

## Develop a Personal Intervention Plan

Once you have admitted your addiction honestly to yourself, you can begin examining how this addiction, or how your codependency, is influencing your classroom instruction. Using the model we suggested previously for helping students, you can set up a personal intervention plan for yourself. Doing this with the help of a counselor or support group will help you be accountable to others and circumvent the temptation to stay in denial.

Build into your personal intervention plan time to reflect on yourself in the classroom. Keep a personal journal to write about your feelings and thoughts relative to your own recovery. Explore in your journal how you think your dysfunctional behaviors are influencing classroom instruction. Be sure to reward yourself for progress you make with your intervention plan.

## Summary

The overall purpose of this chapter is to help you develop an addiction-free classroom. Removing addiction from your classroom means freeing your classroom learning environment from the many behaviors that you and your students exhibit from consuming licit and illicit substances. Having an addiction-free classroom also requires you to remove the enabling and codependent behaviors that may be setting an inappropriate tone for learning. Striving for an addiction-free classroom requires you to thoughtfully reflect and proactively think about your teaching. Because as many as one fourth of the students in your classroom(s) are from homes ruled by addiction, and because just as many early adolescent and high school students are socially using, if not abusing, substances, striving for an addiction-free classroom is not just another idealistic initiative. It is an educational imperative.

# 9

# Searching for Balance: Confronting Our Own Addictions

Although this book is about the influence of addiction on your classroom, it is also about how your life experiences in the past affect what you are doing in the present. We began the book by drawing from our own experiences as children who lived under the influence of our parents' addictions, as well as our professional lives as educators. We intend to close just as we began.

As we progress to the end of our discussion, we wish to extend the biographies of addiction that we began in the first chapter. We move our stories beyond our adolescent years and highlight how growing up within addictive home environments has fostered our professional accomplishments while creating lifelong challenges for our personal lives. Following our lead, we then ask you to explore your own personal biography. Drawing from recent work on the personal lives of teachers, we then consider the notion of personal narratives and what this means for your teaching. We conclude the book with a summary checklist of what you can do to counteract the forces of addiction that are always at work to keep your classroom under the influence.

## Biographies of Addiction: A Continuation

### Richard Powell

I began college the fall semester after completing high school; I graduated in the lower one third of my high school class. Whereas some of my peers were attending large state universities, and a few went out of state to attend prestigious private schools, I began college across the street from my home at a local community college.

During my first semester at college, I started a life of compulsive overachievement, of extreme work habits, and for many years, of living a life out of control. It was also during that same time that the survival strategies I learned at home came to fruition; they took over, and I developed a momentum for my life that none of my high school teachers could have predicted. Indeed, I remember very clearly during my senior year that one of my teachers had asked each one of us in class what we planned to do the following year. When I said I wanted to attend college, he looked directly at me and said without any hesitation, "You'll never make it, Powell. Better look for something else."

I have very few fond memories of my high school years, perhaps a function of trying to survive the constant embarrassment and shame I experienced from living with an alcoholic. College, however, was very different for me. I was freed from the grade point tracking that predominated social groups in high school, and I wasn't surrounded daily by my father's drunkenness. By then, he and mother had separated, my sister had gone to college out of town, and I was living in a more serene environment.

College became a refuge; it also was the fertile ground for cultivating some of the survival strategies I learned growing up with an alcoholic father and codependent mother. Until then, however, these survival strategies were yet in a seed stage, and I was unaware of their potential for my life; the community college I attended for a year helped the survival strategies germinate, and the university setting brought them to full bloom.

When I began college, I recall very clearly being intrinsically motivated to do well, something that I totally lacked in high school. I wanted to excel in my work, to make Mother proud of me, and to show others that I could succeed: what my high school, with its tracking, peer pressure, and teacher indifference, seemed to stifle. I defined excellence in college as making straight As, and because the lower high school track I was in didn't contain college preparatory courses, I found myself working twice as hard as others to make the same grades.

Making the dean's honor roll my first semester in college added more fuel to my motivation to work hard, to spend excessive hours poring over books, memorizing every word if necessary to maintain high grades. This, then, was the beginning of what became a life of compulsive work habits, of a never-ending search for ways to improve my self-esteem. Through achievement in college, I tried to rid myself of the embarrassment I felt about my father and to help my mother realize her dream of a college education for her son.

College, then, became my refuge, my comfort zone, and my way of proving to the world that somehow my life at home was not as bad as it appeared. However, the process I established for myself became more than a means to an end. School became my existence—it was how I defined myself, how I tried to rid myself of shame and embarrassment. Straight As, the dean's honor list, and being in honor clubs were the tokens that appeared to remove the shame and that provided me with a positive self-image; for the first time, I really felt good about myself. Underneath all this, however, remained a fragile self-image and a very low self-confidence.

I graduated from the university and became a science teacher. I then began work on a graduate degree in biology while I was teaching. In the midst of these graduate studies, I spent every night preparing lesson plans, grading papers, and getting ready to teach the next day. In the face of my compulsive work habits and my internal drive to be perfect in my schoolwork, I gave very little time to building family relationships, attending social functions, or cultivating friendships. I completed my master's degree in biology with straight As and continued teaching in secondary school for several years. Yet my need to boost my self-esteem with excellent schoolwork, my latent desire to live out my mother's dream for her son, and my need to rescue my family from shame and embarrassment provided some of the incentives to pursue a doctoral degree.

My obsession with work, my unharnessed compulsive work ethic, and my seemingly unending drive caused ongoing problems in other areas of my life. Issues of intimacy, jealousy, control, and compulsivity interfered with my first marriage, which ended after 8 years. Fifteen years later, as I write this biographical account of my life, these issues are still with me, although they exist in a more manageable form.

Throughout all this, however, I've succeeded in my professional life. I feel good about my accomplishments, in spite of the difficulties they have created for me personally. I am aware of my life, my existence, more now than at any other time. Yet this awareness does not make the path any less arduous.

I know that my life growing up with an alcoholic father and a codependent mother shaped me into who I am now; I know that as an adult I am responsible for my actions and their implications. Yet I constantly wonder how my life might have been different had I spent my formative years in a home filled with explicit love, support, and ongoing kindness, rather than a home filled with uncertainty, where each of us had to learn to survive in different ways. I also wonder, in a very curious way, whether I would have been able to achieve in academic life had I not acquired the compulsive drive that seems to be an ever-present part of my life, that seems to move me forward in often unpredictable ways.

I eventually became the dutiful son who would lift my family, and its image, to higher standards. As much as my father was determined to be a drunk, I was determined to be a family hero. As much as he squandered money on booze and women, I have focused on becoming a perfect worker. As much as my father brought embarrassment and shame to my mother, sister, and me, I've sought to bring pride and praise. In doing these things I've become, like my father, an addict; his booze has become my work; his drunken breath has become my computer keyboard and word processor; and while he tried to drown his pain and anger with booze, I've done the same with accomplishments, awards, and degrees.

Reflecting on the relationship between my dysfunctional behaviors and my former and present teaching, I feel I was and am successful because of my propensity to give myself entirely to my work. Not only are excessively detailed lesson plans, instructional activities, and extracurricular activities part of my regular teaching, so, too, is my interaction with students. Wanting to succeed in every part of my teaching, I have focused intensely on meeting students' needs, developing activities that challenge them, and continuously encouraging them to do well. I have remained sensitive to students who have special personal needs, and I recall meeting with high school students on many occasions after school to talk about their personal problems. This does not mean, however, that my teaching has been free of errors. Indeed, I've made lots of mistakes over these past years in various classroom settings. Because I am obsessed with perfectionism, however, these errors constantly threaten my esteem and confidence. With all this preoccupation on being a "perfect" teacher, and with the constant threat of making personal mistakes, my teaching then has always been, and remains, under the influence of both my father's and my own addictions.

Six years have passed since I began, in earnest, a personal recovery program. During this time, which has seen many ups and downs, I've tried to understand what it means to have balance in life, to do something besides compulsively work 14, 15, 16 hours a day. Only recently have I begun to enrich my life with deeper friendships, with personal intimacy, and with trust-filled relationships. Although I'm beginning to feel more alive than ever before, I'm very aware that I'm yet on a tightrope, trying to resist the gravity of compulsive behaviors that continuously pull me into self-abusive behaviors. My work, my writing, is still an obsession for me, but it has now become more enjoyable as I mix it with time spent with friends and family, and with hiking in nearby canyons.

**Stanley Zehm**

Adult individuals, whose families of origin were filled with the trauma of family addiction, frequently find professional successes that mask the continuing pain and anxiety of their personal lives. I know: I am one of them. Professional achievement, as I shared with you in the beginning of my story, was another strategy I used to hide my pain, pretend I was personally fit, and deny the dysfunctions of my family of origin.

My need to find personal healing was literally brought home to me by my wife. She was the one person I could not hide from; she knew my story. Her own story was similar to mine because she also was raised in an alcoholic family. Fortunately, she realized her need to establish a personal program of recovery and found the help she needed to begin to reclaim her life. After she began her own program of recovery, my wife confronted me with a challenge I could not ignore. "Either we get healthy, rebuild our relationship, and end our family cycle of addiction, or we terminate our marriage. Now!"

I genuinely loved my wife. I did not want to end our marriage and disrupt our family life, dysfunctional though it was. So, with a great deal of initial reluctance, I began my own program of personal therapy. During my weekly individual counseling sessions, I learned to understand the effects of my growing up in an alcoholic family. I learned to recognize how my actions as an individual person, husband, and father were still influenced by the dependent programming I received in my toxic family living. I recognized how my drive toward perfectionism and my controlling behaviors were interfering in my relationships with my wife, children, friends, and colleagues.

With the assistance of my counselor, I examined the painful experiences of my childhood I had repressed. I confronted my father with the burden of pain and shame I had been carrying within me all of those years . . . and I forgave him.

Family therapy sessions also gave me the support I needed to share my story with my wife and children. These sessions taught me how to communicate my innermost feelings to them. They also helped my family realize how many of my behaviors toward them were shaped by my dysfunctional upbringing.

These sessions gave us the hope that we could end this cycle of addicted family living with our family.

I also began attending an all-male therapy group during this time. The group was composed of men whose lives, like my own, were affected by living in a dependent situation with an alcoholic parent or spouse. I'll never forget the first session I went to. I wasn't too excited about going. It was one thing dealing with my depressing family history with a professional counselor in a confidential setting. It was quite another thing to reveal my pain and shame to a group of strangers.

During that first session, I listened quietly as the male participants identified themselves by their first names and began to tell their stories. At first, I thought that my wife had called them and told them my story because each contributor revealed part of the narrative of my personal family struggle. I began to realize that there were many people like me whose childhood was diminished by the pain and shame of living in an alcoholic family.

It has been 12 years since I began my personal program of recovery. I still have to work at not succumbing to the old behaviors. But I am much happier today than I have ever been in my life. I possess an inner serenity that has enabled me to put my childhood into perspective. I now appreciate the anguish my parents suffered in their attempts to provide for their family. I can even appreciate my father in a way that was impossible before.

## Jeffrey Kottler

I don't feel much like a victim—of addiction, a toxic family, or anything else. I believe that my parents did the best that they could. For me. For my brothers. For themselves. That it wasn't good enough is too damn bad. I don't like looking over my shoulder; I then tend to miss what lies ahead. This is not denial. It is acceptance.

I was a wreck as an adolescent. I definitely felt responsible for my parents' divorce, my mother's depression, and my father's absence. In my senior year, I bailed out of my mother's home to live with my father. I still feel bad about leaving my brothers to fend for themselves, but I had to do something to save myself.

It was about halfway through my sophomore year in college that I finally took charge of my life. I had been a mediocre student until that point. In fact, I had been spectacularly undistinguished in anything I ever did (although I once set the camp record for sit-ups, an accomplishment that allowed me to feel special for an hour until someone else broke the record). I decided I was tired of being invisible. Until this point, about the only way that I stood out among my friends was in my steadfast refusal to try drugs of any kind. This was the '60s. Marijuana was as prevalent as tobacco. LSD. Magic Mushrooms. Quaaludes®. Hashish. Thai sticks. It was all around me, yet I was the one who always drove everyone else home. Damn if I was ever going to let a drug, or anything, control me the way it had my mother. And that goes for food as well.

Besides abstaining from intoxication, I discovered another way that I could stand out was to pretend to be smart. I say pretend because I never believed that I was particularly bright (and I still don't). I just work harder than anyone else. I have self-discipline. Or rather, I don't "have" it, I went out and created it in myself. With this single-minded dedication to succeed, I found that I could get what I wanted most of the time. Not the first time, or even the third or fourth. But I am tenacious and I will stick with it until I succeed. I was rejected by over 20 graduate schools before I could find a place that would let me in. My first book was rejected by more than 50 publishers. In a perverse way, I am proud of my perseverance. Anyone with talent can get what they want, but I must be real special if I can get so far with so little going for me.

My brothers are both recovering addicts. They did not escape my mother's legacy that killed her so young. They still attend Alcoholics Anonymous and Narcotics Anonymous meetings several times each week. They live one day at a time, humbled by the realization that any time now they could lose their tenuous illusion of control. There are no support groups for my addiction. Like Richard, I am overdriven to prove that I am not really mediocre.

These past few years I have been turning out books as fast as my fingers can type them, 15, 16, 17, 18, and counting. Whatever I do, it is not enough. No matter how much I am loved by students, I remain focused on the one I could not reach. I am never satisfied with the quality of what I am doing. I could do better. If only I was smarter, more talented, if I didn't have to pretend anymore.

I am not my mother. I am not my mother. This is my mantra. I prove it by taking care of my body, by staying fit and slim, and by eschewing drugs and alcohol. By and large, my addiction to work and compulsive productivity has stayed within reasonable limits, at least in the time I save to be with my family, to travel and hike, and to read novels and play. With the help of some wonderful teachers and therapists along the way, I have been able to channel the legacy of my toxic family into a life that feels quite satisfying. It was the few teachers who saved me. There were a few mentors along the way, one in junior high, one in high school, one in college, and one in graduate school, who all saw something in me that was worth nurturing. It was their support, their belief in my potential, and their caring that prodded me to escape my mother's fate.

I am a teacher today because it was the teachers who saved me. They showed me a path out of my pain and mediocrity. I owe them big time. The only way I can think to pay them back is to be there for others who are like I used to be. The very purpose and meaning of my life centers around the privilege I feel that perhaps these words, or others that I have spoken earlier, might make a difference to somebody. That is what makes all the suffering worthwhile.

### Personal Narratives

Our stories of addiction suggest the value of looking closely at how personal histories shape our professional lives. As teachers, we need to begin with ourselves, to explore our biographies, and to look at how these histories shape our beliefs, attitudes, values, and interactions with students (Hunt, 1987).

A growing body of research on teachers' lives indicates that our level of personal success in the classroom and our predispositions for working with students are influenced in important ways by our biographies and personal narratives. These narratives are intertwined with, and inseparable from, the learning environments you create for students. Your learning environment and your classroom curriculum are socially constructed as you interact with students individually and as a group. However, your learning environment is overshadowed by the personal features you bring to the classroom (see Bullough, 1989; Connelly & Clandinin, 1990; Goodson, 1990; Knowles, 1988; Powell, in press).

As a teacher, you have a story to tell about yourself and how your personal life and prior experiences outside of school became part of your teaching style. By looking closely at yourself, by studying your own teaching through various reflective processes, you can begin to learn about how prior and existing experiences outside school influence your interactions with students in subtle yet profound ways. This is especially crucial if you were, or still are, living in an addictive environment outside school. Writing your biography, and exploring factors that influence your interaction with students, is an important step to counteracting the forces of addiction in your classroom.

Our stories end here. Your story is just beginning. We urge you to write your own narrative, either on paper, in your head, or better yet, to an audience of trusted peers. It is by telling our personal stories that we come to accept the parts of us that we have inherited from the past and, more important, are able to rewrite those chapters for which we would like different endings.


### Final Checklist: Overcoming the Influence of Addiction

No matter how knowledgeable you become about addiction, no matter how deeply you explore your personal biography to discover its influence on your teaching, and no matter how skilled you become in recognizing students who live with addicts or who are themselves addicted to substances, the addiction phenomenon will always be rubbing against your classroom learning environment. Yet by gaining addiction literacy, you can minimize the effects of addiction on your teaching, on your interactions with students, and on student learning.

We have talked about many aspects of addiction throughout this book relative to your classroom teaching. We have shared with you our stories of addiction. We have also highlighted the special challenges that students from addictive environments have for your classroom teaching, and we have offered suggestions for what to do and what not to do for these students. We would like to complete our discussion of addiction by summarizing five key points for counteracting the forces of addiction in your classroom.

1. *Explore the relationship between your personal biography and your classroom learning environment.* Recent studies on teacher biography suggest that when you began teaching, you lacked a clear image of yourself as a professional; you were unaware of how your personal biography influenced your classroom instruction (e.g., Bullough, 1989). Little effort was made in helping you develop these understandings if you completed a teacher preparation program that placed greater emphasis on the technical skills of teaching (e.g., developing objectives, making lesson plans) than on helping you become a reflective, caring practitioner (Zehm & Kottler, 1993). Although developing and refining technical skills is an important part of teaching, so is knowing about the relationship between self, biography, and learning environment.

2. *Learn about the addiction phenomenon.* The addiction phenomenon is pervasive. It touches everyone. Knowing how you and your classroom are influenced by the addiction phenomenon can help you develop insight into students' lives, into your relationship with selected students, and how you might overcome some of the problems you are experiencing. Through this process you will begin moving your classroom toward an addiction-free environment.

3. *Reflect on your classroom learning environment.* In the busy happenings of the daily classroom, it is hard to take a few minutes just to think about your day and to ask reflective questions about your teaching and about your interactions

with students. The pressures of the day keep you on task almost every minute. Yet just a few minutes of reflective thinking about your teaching, when done in solitude, can be refreshing. Such introspective study can provide you with insight and can help you understand the relationship between addiction and your teaching.

4. *Develop a helping, caring classroom curriculum.* You might already have a classroom environment where students feel secure, trusted, and cared for. This is exactly the kind of curriculum that helps children of addicts in school. We know it is not always easy to extend a helping hand to students who constantly act out, who threaten the tranquility of your learning environment. Indeed, children of addicts and children who are becoming substance abusers will challenge your patience as a teacher. We are also aware that extending yourself too much, becoming preoccupied with nurturing students, can wear you out emotionally.

5. *Don't feel that you have to deal with the addiction phenomenon alone.* We encourage you to seek out the help of other professionals when you need specialized help with students. For many students of addicts, you will be able to provide special assistance in your classroom in small but significant ways; for some, however, special help may be needed. Other teachers, school counselors, and administrators who are familiar with addiction may be in positions to provide you with the assistance you need.

## Summary

Although we have an insider's view of the addiction phenomenon, and although we know firsthand what it is like to live with an addict while trying to meet the daily rigors of school, we don't have all the answers to helping every student in your classroom. Nor do we expect you to have all the answers.

One thing we are clear about is that addiction has a profound influence in school classrooms and underlies many other problems you deal with each day of your school life. Our challenge to you is to consider the influence of addiction on your professional life. Do not underestimate the strength of denial, and do realize when you are enabling students to maintain their dysfunctional behaviors in your classroom. Don't expect to save students from the perils of living within an addictive environment, but do expect to help them in subtle ways in your classroom. They need you as a responsible and trusted role model. They need your care, your concern, and your ability to understand their plight. Above all, they need to know they are understood and that their cries for help, however subtle or however explicit, are heard.

# References

Ackerman, R. J. (1987). *Children of alcoholics: A guide for parents, educators, and therapists.* New York: Simon & Schuster.

American Psychiatric Association. (1994). *Diagnostic and statistical manual of mental disorders* (4th ed.). Washington, DC: Author.

Baird, M. (1991). Care of family members and other affected persons. In M. Fleming & K. Barry (Eds.), *Addictive disorders.* Boston: Mosby-Year Book.

Berkowitz, A., & Perkins, H. W. (1988). Personality characteristics of children of alcoholics. *Journal of Consulting and Clinical Psychology, 56*(2), 206-209.

Berlin, R., Davis, R. B., & Orenstein, A. (1988). Adaptive and reactive distancing among adolescents from alcoholic families. *Adolescence, 23,* 577-584.

Black, C. (1979). Children of alcoholics. *Alcohol Health and Research World, 4*(1), 23-27.

Bowen, M. (1982). *Family therapy in clinical practice.* New York: Aronson.

Bullough, R. V. (1989). *First year teacher: A case study.* New York: Teachers College Press.

Connelly, F. M., & Clandinin, D. J. (1990). Stories of experience and narrative inquiry. *Educational Researcher, 19*(5), 2-14.

Dean, O. A. (1989). *Facing chemical dependency in the classroom.* Deerfield Beach, FL: Health Communications.

Deutsch, C. (1982). *Broken bottles, broken dreams: Understanding and helping the children of alcoholics.* New York: Teachers College Press.

Donovan, D. M. (1988). Assessment of addictive behaviors. In D. M. Donovan & G. A. Marlatt (Eds.), *Assessment of addictive behaviors* (pp. 3-48). New York: Guilford.

El-Guebaly, N., & Offord, D. (1977). The offspring of alcoholics: A critical review. *American Journal of Psychiatry, 134*(4), 357-364.

Faraco-Hadlock, G. (1990). Adolescent depression and substance abuse. *Journal of Psychology and Christianity, 9*(4), 64-71.

Forward, S. (1989). *Toxic parents.* New York: Bantam Books.

Gabe, J. (1989). *A professional's guide to adolescent substance abuse.* Springfield, IL: Academy of Addictions Treatment Professionals.

Goldenberg, I., & Goldenberg, H. (1991). *Family therapy: An overview.* Pacific Grove, CA: Brooks/Cole.

Goodson, I. (1990). Studying curriculum: Towards a social constructionist perspective. *Journal of Curriculum Studies, 22*(4), 299-312.

Haley, J. (1976). *Problem solving therapy.* New York: Harper & Row.

Hernandez, J. T. (1992). Substance abuse among sexually abused adolescents and their families. *Journal of Adolescent Health, 13,* 658-662.

Hunt, D. (1987). *Beginning with ourselves.* Cambridge, MA: Brookline Press.

Jacobs, J., & Wolin, S. J. (1991). *Resilient children growing up in alcoholic families.* Paper presented at the National Consensus Symposium on CoAs and Codependence, Airlie Conference Center, Airlie, VA.

Johnston, L. D., & O'Malley, P. M. (1986). Why do the nation's students use drugs and alcohol? Self-reported reasons from nine national surveys. *The Journal of Drug Issues, 16,* 29-66.

Kaufman, E. (1985). *Substance abuse and family therapy.* New York: Grune & Stratton.

Knowles, G. (1988, April). *Models for understanding preservice and beginning teachers' biographies: Illustrations from case studies*. Paper presented at the annual meeting of the American Educational Research Association, New Orleans, LA.

Kottler, J. A. (1990). *Private moments secret selves: Enriching our time alone*. New York: Ballantine.

Kottler, J. A. (1991). *The compleat therapist*. San Francisco: Jossey-Bass.

Kottler, J. A. (1992). *Compassionate therapy: Working with difficult clients*. San Francisco: Jossey-Bass.

Kottler, J. A. (1993). *On being a therapist* (2nd ed.). San Francisco: Jossey-Bass.

Kottler, J. A. (1994). *Beyond blame: A new way of resolving conflict in relationships*. San Francisco: Jossey-Bass.

Kottler, J. A., and Blau, D. (1989). *The imperfect therapist: Learning from failure in therapeutic practice*. San Francisco: Jossey-Bass.

Kottler, J. A., & Brown, R.W. (1992). *Introduction to therapeutic counseling* (2nd ed.). Pacific Grove, CA: Brooks/Cole.

Kottler, J. A., & Kottler, E. (1993). *Teacher as counselor: Developing the helping skills you need*. Newbury Park, CA: Corwin.

Kottler, J. A., & Zehm, S. (1993). Solitude: A resource for active student learning. *People and Education, 1*(3), 196-202.

Kozol, J. (1991). *Savage inequalities: Children in America's Schools*. New York: Crown.

Kritsberg, W. (1986). *The adult children of alcoholics syndrome*. Pompano Beach, FL: Health Communications.

Landfried, S. E. (1990). Educational enabling: Is "helping" hurting our students? *Middle School Journal, 21*(5), 12-15.

Lewis, J. A., Dana, R. Q., & Blevins, G. A. (1994). *Substance abuse counseling: An individualized approach* (2nd ed.). Pacific Grove, CA: Brooks/Cole.

Madanes, C. (1983). *Strategic family therapy*. San Francisco: Jossey-Bass.

Madanes, C. (1990). *Love, sex, and violence*. New York: Norton.

Maslach, C. (1986). *Stress, burnout, and alcoholism*. In R. R. Kilburg, P. E. Nathan, & R. W. Thoreson (Eds.), *Professionals in distress* (pp. 53-76). Washington, DC: American Psychological Association.

McAndrew, J. A. (1985). Children of alcoholics: School intervention. *Childhood Education, 615*, 343-345.

McKay, J. R., Murphy, R. T., McGuire, J., Rivinus, T. R., & Maisto, S. A. (1992). Incarcerated adolescents attributions for drug and alcohol use. *Addictive Behaviors, 17*, 227-235.

Metzger, L., (1988). *From denial to recovery: Counseling problem drinkers, alcoholics, and their families*. San Francisco: Jossey-Bass.

Minuchin, S. (1974). *Families and family therapy*. Cambridge, MA: Harvard University Press.

Novacek, J., Raskin, R., & Hogan, R. (1991). Why do adolescents use drugs? Age, sex, and user differences. *Journal of Youth and Adolescence, 20*(5), 475-491.

Powell, R. R. (in press). Prior experiences, instructional tasks, and classroom climate: A qualitative study of second-career secondary student teachers. *International Journal of Qualitiative Studies in Education.*

Powell, R. R., Gabe, J., & Zehm, S. J. (1994). *Classrooms under the influence: Helping early adolescent children of alcoholics*. Reston, VA: National Association of Secondary School Principals.

Powell, R. R., & Zehm, S. (1991). Classrooms under the influence: Helping early adolescent children of alcoholics. *Schools in the Middle*, 6-11.

Priest, K. (1985). Adolescents' response to parents' alcoholism. *The Journal of Contemporary Social Work, 66*(9), 533-539.

Reynolds, J. (1987). Our unknown students: Children/teens of alcoholics. *Momentum, 18*(3), 42-43.

Sanders, S. R. (1989, November). Under the influence: Paying the price of my father's booze. *Harper's Magazine*, pp. 68-75.

Satir, V. (1967). *Conjoint family therapy*. Palo Alto, CA: Science & Behavior Books.

Scales, P. (1990). Developing capable young people: An alternative strategy for prevention programs. *Journal of Early Adolescence, 10*(4), 420-438.

Segal, B. (1991). Adolescent initiation into drug-taking behavior: Comparisons over a 5-year interval. *The International Journal of Addictions, 26*(3), 267-279.

Steinglass, P., Bennett, L., Wolin, S., & Reiss, D. (1987). *The Alcoholic Family*. New York: Basic Books.

Storti, E., & Keller, J. (1988). *Crisis intervention: Acting against addiction*. New York: Crown.

Tharinger, D. J., & Koranek, M. E. (1988). Children of alcoholics, at risk and unserved: A review of research and service roles for school psychologists. *School Psychology Review, 17*(1), 166-191.

Towers, R. L. (1989). *Children of alcoholics/addicts.* Washington, DC: National Education Association.

Treadway, D. (1989). *Before its too late: Working with substance abuse in the family.* New York: Norton.

Veenam, S. (1984). Perceived problems of beginning teachers. *Review of Educational Research, 54*(2), 143-178.

Walter, H. J., Vaughan, R. D., & Cohall, A.T. (1991). Risk factors for substance use among high school students: Implications for prevention. *Journal of the American Academy of Child Adolescent Psychiatry, 30*(4), 556-562.

Wegscheider, S. (1981). *Another chance: Hope and health for the alcoholic family.* Palo Alto, CA: Science & Behavior Books.

Weil, A. (1972). *The natural mind.* Boston: Houghton-Mifflin.

Wodarski, J. S. (1990). Adolescent substance abuse: Practice implications. *Adolescence, 25*(99), 667-688.

Zehm, S. J., & Kottler, J. A. (1993). *On being a teacher: The human dimension.* Newbury Park, CA: Corwin.

Zelvin, E. (1993). Treating partners of substance abusers. In S. L. Straussner (Ed.), *Clinical work with substance abusing clients* (pp. 196-213). New York: Guilford.